T0114405

"Malcolm analyzes the transformations that Chekhov grants his redeemable roués and guileless heroines, and illuminates the hidden surreality and waywardness of his realism."
　—*The New Yorker*

"Her method is that of the careful reporter who, in Chekhovian manner, starts out with quotidian details, small particulars of time and place . . . and, giving credit to other critics, where it is due, builds on her observations and recollections of the stories and plays to reach heights of feeling and judgment."
　—Washington, D.C., *Sunday Times*

"*Reading Chekhov: A Critical Journey* brings the Russian master under the gaze of an astute journalist and critic."
　—*Newsday* (one of *Newsday*'s Favorite Books of 2001)

"Part literary appreciation, part biography, part travelogue as Malcolm visits Chekhov's various Russian haunts, it's a lush, thoughtful and beautifully written consideration of the premier practitioner of the [short story] form."
　—*The Orlando Sentinel*

". . . informative and beautifully written."
　—*Time Out New York*

"[Malcolm] seamlessly stitches together both standard bio-graphical information . . . and close analysis and interpretation. . . . Malcolm offers a stirring, roving chronicle of 'our poet of the provisional and fragmentary.' "
    —*Kirkus Reviews*

"Malcolm . . . brings her considerable talents to Chekhov studies in a work that is a combination of biography, travel book, and literary criticism. . . . In each chapter, she deftly takes us back to Chekhov's day. . . . It is not necessary to know Chekhov's writings to enjoy this splendid book, but it will serve to prod the reader to Chekhov's works and the treasures that await."
    —*Library Journal*

"*Reading Chekhov* is brilliantly composed and a delight to read."
    —*The Sunday Oregonian*

"Malcolm's thinking about Chekhov is clear and her writing is always good, often exceptional—stylistically worthy, in short, of her subject. . . . Malcolm's biggest achievement is that she directs you back to the author—a refreshing change from the critics who want to direct you to themselves, their colleagues and their jargon."
    —Madison, Wisconsin, *Capital Times*

"Janet Malcolm's *Reading Chekhov* was fluent and engaging, testifying to, apart from everything else, the great affection and instinctive regard so many writers . . . have felt towards the Russian genius."
    —*Times Literary Supplement* (one of *TLS*'s International Books of the Year)

PHOTO © ALLAN MILLER

JANET MALCOLM'S previous books are *Diana and Nikon: Essays on Photography*; *Psychoanalysis: The Impossible Profession*; *In the Freud Archives*; *The Journalist and the Murderer*; *The Purloined Clinic: Selected Writings*; *The Silent Woman: Sylvia Plath and Ted Hughes*; and *The Crime of Sheila McGough*. Born in Prague, she grew up in New York, where she lives with her husband, Gardner Botsford.

Reading Chekhov

Anton Chekhov

READING
CHEKHOV

A Critical Journey

JANET
MALCOLM

RANDOM HOUSE

TRADE PAPERBACKS

NEW YORK

Grateful acknowledgment is made to the following for permission to reprint previously
published material:

Ivan R. Dee, Publisher: Excerpt from *Chekhov: The Hidden Ground* by Philip Callow.
Copyright © 1998 by Philip Callow. Reprinted by permission of Ivan R. Dee, Publisher.

Alfred A. Knopf, a division of Random House, Inc.: Excerpt from "Where I'm Calling
From" from *Cathedral* by Raymond Carver. Copyright © 1983 by Raymond Carver.
Reprinted by permission of Alfred A. Knopf, a division of Random House, Inc.

Northwestern University Press: Excerpt from *Reading Chekhov's Text* by Robert Louis
Jackson (Evanston, IL: Northwestern University Press, 1993). Copyright © 1993 by
Northwestern University Press. Reprinted by permission of Northwestern University Press.

Zephyr Press: Excerpt from "Requiem" from *The Complete Poems of Anna Akhmatova,*
translated by Judith Hemschemeyer, edited by Robert Reeder. Copyright © 1989 by Judith
Hemschemeyer. Reprinted by permission of Zephyr Press.

Library of Congress Cataloging-in-Publication Data
Malcolm, Janet.
Reading Chekhov / Janet Malcolm.
p.   cm.
ISBN 978-0-375-76106-5
1. Chekhov, Anton Pavlovich, 1860–1904—Criticism and interpretation. I. Title.
PG3458.Z8 M28   2001   891.72'3—dc21   2001019585

Random House website address: www.atrandom.com

TO GARDNER

What torture it is to cut the nails on your right hand!

Chekhov, letter to Olga Knipper,
October 30, 1903

Reading Chekhov

One

After they have slept together for the first time, Dmitri Dmitrich Gurov and Anna Sergeyevna von Diderits, the hero and heroine of Anton Chekhov's story "The Lady with the Dog" (1899), drive out at dawn to a village near Yalta called Oreanda, where they sit on a bench near a church and look down on the sea. "Yalta was hardly visible through the morning mist; white clouds stood motionless on the mountain-tops," Chekhov writes at the start of the famous passage that continues:

> The leaves did not stir on the trees, grasshoppers chirruped, and the monotonous hollow sound of the sea rising up from below, spoke of the peace, of the eternal sleep awaiting us. So it must have sounded when there was no Yalta, no Oreanda here; so it sounds now, and it will sound as indifferently and monotonously when we are all no more. And in this constancy, in this complete indifference to the life and

death of each of us, there lies hid, perhaps, a pledge of our eternal salvation, of the unceasing movement of life upon earth, of unceasing progress towards perfection. Sitting beside a young woman who in the dawn seemed so lovely, soothed and spellbound in these magical surroundings—the sea, mountains, clouds, the open sky—Gurov thought how in reality everything is beautiful in this world when one reflects: everything except what we think or do ourselves when we forget our human dignity and the higher aims of our existence.

Today, I am sitting on that same bench near the church looking at the same view. Beside me is my English-speaking guide Nina (I know no Russian), and a quarter of a mile away a driver named Yevgeny waits in his car at the entrance of the footpath leading to the lookout point where Gurov and Anna sat, not yet aware of the great love that lay before them. I am a character in a new drama: the absurdist farce of the literary pilgrim who leaves the magical pages of a work of genius and travels to an "original scene" that can only fall short of his expectations. However, because Nina and Yevgeny have gone to some trouble to find the spot, I pretend to be thrilled by it. Nina—a large woman in her late sixties, with short, straight blond hair, forget-me-not blue eyes, and an open passionate nature—is gratified. She breaks into song. "It's a big, wide wonderful world that we live in," she sings, and then asks, "Do you know this song?" When I say I do, she tells me that Deanna Durbin sang it in the 1948 film *For the Love of Mary*.

"Do you like Deanna Durbin?" she asks. I say yes.

"I adore Deanna Durbin," Nina says. "I have adored her since I was a girl."

She tells me of a chance encounter in a church in Yalta, two years earlier, with an Englishwoman named Muriel, who turned out to be another adorer of Deanna Durbin, and who subsequently invited her to the annual conference of an organization called the Deanna Durbin Society, which was held that year in Scarborough, England. Nina owns videos of all of Deanna Durbin's movies and knows all the songs Deanna Durbin sang. She offers to give me the address of the Deanna Durbin Society.

Nina was born and educated in St. Petersburg and, after studying languages at the university there, became an In-tourist guide, presently moving to Yalta. She has retired, and, like most retirees in the former Soviet Union, she cannot live on her pension. She now hires out as an independent guide and waits for assignments from the Hotel Yalta, currently the only habitable hotel in the town. My trip to Yalta is a stroke of good fortune for her; she had not worked for a long time when the call from the hotel came.

It is the second day of my acquaintance with Nina, the third day of my stay at the Hotel Yalta, and the ninth day of my trip to the former Soviet Union. I have worked my way south from St. Petersburg and Moscow. My arrival in Yalta was marked by an incident that rather dramatically brought into view something that had lain just below my consciousness as I pursued my itinerary of visits to houses where Chekhov lived and places he had written about. I had flown from Moscow to Simferopol, the nearest town to Yalta with an airport, a two-hour drive away. Chekhov lived in Yalta during much of the last five years of his life. (He died in July 1904.) At that time, exile to places with mild climates, like the Crimea and the Riviera, was the favored therapy for tuberculosis, into whose last stages Chekhov was entering in the late 1890s. He built a handsome villa a few miles outside the city center, in a suburb called Autka, and also bought a small cottage on the water in a seaside Tatar village called Gurzuv. He wrote *Three Sisters* and *The Cherry Orchard,* as well as "The Lady with the Dog" and "The Bishop," in these houses.

At the Simferopol airport, as I stood in line at the immigration counter waiting to have my passport and visa stamped, I saw, as if in a dream's slow motion, a man in the baggage area on the other side of a glass panel walk out of the building with my suitcase in his hand. The hallucination proved to be real. In a daze, I filled out a lost luggage form and followed an English-speaking woman who worked for the Hotel Yalta to a car in the parking lot. She said she would trace my luggage and disappeared. The driver—the same Yevgeny who now sits in the car in Oreanda—drove me to the hotel in silence, his English and my Russian in exact equilibrium.

As we neared the Black Sea coast, the Ukrainian farm country gave way to a terrain resembling—and, in the variety and beauty of its vegetation, surpassing—that of the Riviera corniches. The winding road offered views of mountains and glimpses of the sea below. But when the Hotel Yalta came into view I caught my breath at its spectacular ugliness. It is a monstrous building—erected in 1975, with a capacity of twenty-five hundred people—that is like a brute's blow in the face of the countryside. Its scale would be problematic anywhere, and on the hillside above Yalta it is catastrophic. Hundreds of—possibly a thousand—identical balconies jut out from a glass and concrete facade. The approach is an American supermarket-style parking lot. The vast, low-ceilinged lobby, with black marble floors and metallic walls, looks as if a failing bank had been crossed with a seedy nightclub. In one corner there is a bar and along one wall stands a row of slot machines. A great expanse of empty black marble floor lies between the slot machines and the hotel's front desk. When I entered the lobby it was almost completely empty: two or three men were playing the slot machines and a couple sat at the bar. At the reception desk, I was given a key to a room on the fourth floor, and, after walking down an almost satirically long empty corridor, I opened the door to a cubicle about eight feet by twelve, pleasingly furnished in the blond-wood Scandina-vian Modern style of the fifties and sixties, and affording just enough room for a double bed, a small round table with two chairs, an armchair, and a minuscule refrigerator. My little balcony—like its myriad replicas—offered a glimpse of the sea and a view of large swimming pools, tennis courts, various outbuildings, and an auditorium. No one was in the pools or on the courts, but American popular music blared out of a loudspeaker. I shut the glass door to muffle the sound and hopefully opened the refrigerator. It was empty. In the bathroom I found serviceable fixtures and a soap dish of plastic made to resemble brown marble.

On my arrival, an unsmiling young man named Igor, who spoke fluent English, had approached me in the lobby and led me to his office, where he enumerated the activities that had been arranged for the next two days with Nina and Yevgeny. These had been prepaid, and he wanted me to un-derstand that anything more would cost extra. (The trip to Oreanda would be one such addition.) When I mentioned my lost luggage and asked if there was somewhere I could buy a nightgown and a change of clothes, he looked at his watch and said that if I walked down to the town—a twenty- or thirty-minute walk—I might still find some cloth-ing stores open.

As I walked to the town in the late-afternoon sunlight, down a winding road fragrant with the smells of the trees and shrubs and wildflowers that lined it, and left the horrible hotel behind, I felt a stir of happiness. Though it was May, St. Petersburg had been icily wintry and Moscow only a few degrees warmer. But here it was true spring; the air was fresh and soft. In a few months—I knew from "The Lady with the Dog"—Yalta would be hot and dusty. On the day Gurov and Anna became lovers "it was sultry indoors, while in the street the wind whirled the dust round and round and blew people's hats off. It was a thirsty day, and Gurov often went into the pavilion, and pressed Anna Sergeyevna to have syrup and water or an ice. One did not know what to do with oneself." In the evening, after mingling with a crowd at the harbor that has gathered to meet a ship coming in, Gurov kisses Anna and they go to her hotel. After they have made love, Anna sits dejected "like 'the woman who was a sinner' in an old fashioned picture," and Gurov callously cuts himself a slice of watermelon and eats it "without haste." Gurov's unforgettable gesture—the mark of the cold roué that he is—only deepens the mystery and heightens the poignancy of his later transformation into a man capable of serious love.

As I walked on, small village houses of a familiar old sort began to appear. Yalta seemed untouched by the hands that had heaved my monstrous hotel into the hillside above it. Along the seafront, some changes had of course taken place since Gurov and Anna strolled there. In the square opposite the harbor stood a huge statue of Lenin gesturing toward the sea; and the harbor itself had become the site of a kiddie park, outfitted with garishly colored cartoon figures. The shops along the tree-lined promenade—selling film and suntan lotion and mermaid dolls and souvenir china—had a neglected, unvisited air; perhaps business would pick up in the hot, dusty season. Many were closed for the day, including the clothing stores. When Chekhov visited Yalta for the first time, in July 1888, he disparaged it thus to his sister Maria: "Yalta is a mixture of something European that reminds one of the views of Nice, with something cheap and shoddy. The box-like hotels in which unhappy consumptives are pining, the impudent Tatar faces, the ladies' bustles with their very undisguised expression of something very abominable, the faces of the idle rich longing for cheap adventures, the smell of perfumery instead of the scent of the cedars and the sea, the miserable dirty pier, the melancholy lights far out at sea, the prattle of young ladies and gentlemen who have crowded here in order to admire nature of which they have no idea—all this taken together produces such a depressing effect and is so overwhelming that one begins to blame oneself for being biased and unfair."

I began my ascent up the hill. The sun was nearing the horizon, and there was a chill in the air. The weight of being thousands of miles from home with nothing to wear but the clothes on my back fell on me. I tried to pull myself together, to rise above my petty obsession with the loss of a few garments, and to that end invoked Chekhov and the heightened sense of what is important in life that gleams out of his work. The shadow of mortality hovers over his texts; his characters repeatedly remind one another, "We all have to die" and "Life is not given twice." Chekhov himself needed no such reminders: the last decade of his life was a daily struggle with increasingly virulent pulmonary and intestinal tuberculosis. And yet when he was dying, in the spa of Badenweiler, where he had stupidly been sent by a specialist, he wrote letters to Maria in which he repeatedly complained not about his fate but about how badly German women dressed. "Nowhere do women dress so abominably. . . . I have not seen one beautiful woman, nor one who was not trimmed with some kind of absurd braid," he wrote on June 8, 1904, and then, on June 28—in his last letter to anyone and his last comment on anything—"There is not a single decently dressed German woman. The lack of taste makes one depressed."

I continued climbing the hill, in the inflexible grip of unhappiness over my lost clothes. And then the realization came: the recognition that when my suitcase was taken something else had been restored to me—*feeling itself*. Until the mishap at the airport, I had not felt anything very much. Without knowing exactly why, I have always found travel writing a little boring, and now the reason seemed clear: travel itself is a low-key emotional experience, a pallid affair in comparison to ordinary life. When Gurov picks up Anna at an outdoor restaurant (approaching her through her dog) they converse thus:

"Have you been long in Yalta?" [he says.]

"Five days."

"And I have already dragged out a fortnight here."
There was a brief silence.

"Time goes fast, and yet it is so dull here!" she said,
not looking at him.

"That's only the fashion to say it is dull here. A
provincial will live in Belyov or Zhidra and not be dull,
and when he comes here it's 'Oh the dullness! Oh, the
dust!' One would think he came from Granada."

Although the passage functions (as Vladimir Nabokov
pointed out) as an illustration of Gurov's attractive wit, it
also expresses the truth that had just been revealed to me,
and that Chekhov's Yalta exile revealed to him—that our
homes are Granada. They are where the action is; they are
where the riches of experience are distributed. On our travels, we stand before paintings and look at scenery, and
sometimes we are moved, but rarely are we as engaged with
life as we are in the course of any ordinary day in our usual
surroundings. Only when faced with one of the inevitable
minor hardships of travel do we break out of the trance of
tourism and once again feel the sharp savor of the real. ("I
have never met anyone who was less a tourist," Maxim Ko-
valevsky, a professor of sociology whom Chekhov met in
Nice in 1897, wrote of his compatriot, and went on to say,

"Visiting museums, art galleries, and ruins exhausted rather than delighted him. . . . In Rome I found myself obliged to assume the role of guide, showing him the Forum, the ruins of the palace of the Caesars, the Capitol. To all of this he remained more or less indifferent.") Chekhov was deeply bored in Yalta before he built his house and put in his garden, and even afterward he felt as if he had been banished and that life was elsewhere. When he wrote of the three sisters' yearning for Moscow, he was expressing his own sense of exile: "One does not know what to do with oneself."

Chekhov's villa in Autka—Nina took me there on our first day together—is a two-story stucco house of distinguished, unornamented, faintly Moorish architecture, with an extensive, well-ordered garden and spacious rooms that look out over Yalta to the sea. Maria Chekhova, who lived until 1957, preserved the house and garden, fending off Nazi occupiers during the war and enduring the insults of the Stalin and Khrushchev periods. It remains furnished as in Chekhov's time: handsomely, simply, elegantly. As Chekhov cared about women's dress (it does not go unnoted in the work, and is always significant), he cared about the furnishings of his houses. Perhaps his love of order and elegance was innate, but more likely it was a reaction against the disorder and harshness of his early family life. His father, Pavel Yegorovich, was the son of a serf who had managed to buy his freedom and that of his wife and children. Pavel rose in the world and became the owner of a grocery store in Taganrog, a town with a large foreign (mostly Greek) population, on the sea of Azov, in southern Russia. The store, as Chekhov's best biographer, Ernest J. Simmons, characterizes it in *Chekhov* (1962), resembled a New England general store—selling things like kerosene, tobacco, yarn, nails, and home remedies—though, unlike a New England store, it also sold vodka, which was consumed on the premises in a separate room. In Simmons's description, the place had "filthy debris on the floor, torn soiled oilcloth on the counters, and in summer, swarms of flies settled everywhere. An unpleasant mélange of odors emanated from the exposed goods: the sugar smelled of kerosene, the coffee of herring. Brazen rats prowled about the stock."

Chekhov's oldest brother, Alexander, in a memoir of Anton, wrote of a freezing winter night on which "the future writer," then a nine-year-old schoolboy, was dragged by his father from the warm room where he was doing his homework and made to mind the unheated store. The account lays stress on the cruelty of the father and the misery of the boy, and is crudely written, in a sort of penny-dreadful style. The reticent Anton himself left no memoir of his childhood sorrows, though there are passages in his stories that are assumed to refer to them. In the long story "Three Years" (1895), for example, the hero, Laptev, says to his wife, "I can remember my father correcting me—or, to speak plainly, beating me—before I was five years old. He used to thrash me with a birch, pull my ears, hit me on the head, and every morning when I woke up my first thought was whether he would beat me that day." In a letter of 1894 to his publisher and close friend Alexei Suvorin, Chekhov permitted himself the bitter reflection, "I acquired my belief in progress when still a child; I couldn't help believing in it, because the difference between the period when they flogged me and the period when they stopped flogging me was enormous." Chekhov had what he described to another correspondent in 1899 as "autobiographophobia." The correspondent was Grigory Rossolimo, who had been a classmate in medical school, and had written to Chekhov to ask him for an autobiography for an album he was assembling for a class reunion—which Chekhov supplied, but not before expressing his reluctance to write about himself. Seven years earlier, when V. A. Tikhonov, the editor of a journal called *Sever,* asked him for biographical information to accompany a photograph, Chekhov made this reply:

> Do you need my biography? Here it is. In 1860 I was born in Taganrog. In 1879 I finished my studies in the Taganrog school. In 1884 I finished my studies in the medical school of Moscow University. In 1888 I received the Pushkin Prize. In 1890 I made a trip to Sakhalin across Siberia—and back by sea. In 1891 I toured Europe, where I drank splendid wine and ate oysters. In 1892 I strolled with V. A. Tikhonov at [the

writer Shcheglov's] name-day party. I began to write in 1879 in *Strekosa.* My collections of stories are *Motley Stories, Twilight, Stories, Gloomy People,* and the novella *The Duel.* I have also sinned in the realm of drama, although moderately. I have been translated into all languages with the exception of the foreign ones. However, I was translated into German quite a while ago. The Czechs and Serbs also approve of me. And the French also relate to me. I grasped the secrets of love at the age of thirteen. I remain on excellent terms with friends, both physicians and writers. I am a bachelor. I would like a pension. I busy myself with medicine to such an extent that this summer I am going to perform some autopsies, something I have not done for two or three years. Among writers I prefer Tolstoy, among physicians, Zakharin. However, this is all rubbish. Write what you want. If there are no facts, substitute something lyrical.

Maxim Gorky wrote of Chekhov that "in the presence of Anton Pavlovich, everyone felt an unconscious desire to be simpler, more truthful, more himself." Chekhov's mock biography produces a similar chastening effect. After reading it, one can only regard any attempt at self-description that is longer and less playful as pretentious and rather ridiculous.

Two

"This morning I felt giddy," Nina tells me at the lookout in Oreanda. "I was afraid I would not be able to come today. Fortunately I am better." I question her about her symptoms and urge her to see a doctor. She explains that she hasn't the money for a doctor—doctors can no longer get by on their salaries from the state and now charge for their services. I ask if there are clinics, and she says yes, but they are overcrowded—one has to wait interminably. She finally agrees to go to a clinic the next day to have her blood pressure checked. Nina and I took to each other immediately. She is extremely likable. Because she is large and I am small she has begun giving me impulsive bear hugs and calling me her little one—for lack of a better equivalent for the Russian diminutive. Over the two days we have been together, I have received an increasing sense of the pathos of her life. She is very poor. Her apartment is too small, she says, to keep a cat in. The dress she is wearing was given to her by a Czech woman whose guide she was a few years ago. She is grateful when clients give her leftover shampoo and hand cream; nothing is too small. Earlier in the day, during a visit to the Livadia palace, where the Yalta agreement was signed, she told me that as a young child she lived through the nine-hundred-day siege of Leningrad. Her grandparents died during the siege, and her parents' lives, she said, were shortened because of the sacrifices they made for their children. Now, as she talks about the leftover shampoo, I think about the large tip I will give her at the end of the day, anticipating her surprise and pleasure. Then a suspicion enters my mind: has she been putting on an act and playing on my sympathy precisely so that I will give her money? A week earlier, in St. Petersburg, someone else had used the term "putting on an act." I had been walking along the Nevsky Prospect with my guide, Nelly, when I was stopped in my tracks by the horrifying sight of an old woman lying face down on the pavement convulsively shaking, a cane on the ground just out of reach of the trembling hand from which it had fallen. As I started to go to her aid, Nelly put her hand on my arm and said, "She lies here like this every day. She is a beggar." She added, "I don't know if she's putting on an act or not." I looked at her in disbelief. "Even if she's acting, she must be in great need," Nelly allowed. I then noticed a paper box with a few coins in it sitting on the ground near the cane. As the occasional passerby added a coin to the box, the woman took no notice; she simply continued to shake.

If Nina is acting, I think, she, too, must be impelled by desperation, but I decide that she is on the level. There is an atmosphere of truth about her. She is like one of Chekhov's guileless innocents; she is Anna Sergeyevna in late middle age. We rise from the seat and walk over to a semicircular stone pavilion at the edge of the cliff. Names and initials have been penciled on or scratched into the stone. In Chekhov's story "Lights" (1888), the hero, an engineer named Ananyev, speaks of a decisive youthful encounter in a stone summerhouse above the sea, and offers this theory of graffiti:

> When a man in a melancholy mood is left tête-à-tête with the sea, or any landscape which seems to him grandiose, there is always, for some reason, mixed with melancholy, a conviction that he will live and die in obscurity and he reflectively snatches up a pencil and hastens to write his name on the first thing that comes handy. And that, I suppose is why all convenient solitary nooks like my summer-house are always scrawled over in pencil or carved with pen-knives.

Ananyev is another of Chekhov's redeemed womanizers, though he undergoes his transformation of soul after hideously betraying the story's gentle, trusting heroine,

Kisotchka. The story was written eleven years before "The Lady with the Dog," and it was not well received. "I was not entirely satisfied with your latest story," the novelist and playwright Ivan Shcheglov wrote to Chekhov on May 29, 1888, and went on:

> Of course, I swallowed it in one gulp, there is no question about that, because everything you write is so appetizing and real that it can be easily and pleasantly swallowed. But that finale—"You can't figure out anything in this world . . ."—is abrupt; it is certainly the writer's job to figure out what goes on in the heart of his hero, otherwise his psychology will remain unclear.

Chekhov replied, on June 9:

> I take the liberty of disagreeing with you. A psychologist should not pretend to understand what he does not understand. Moreover, a psychologist should not convey the impression that he understands what no one understands. We shall not play the charlatan, and we will declare frankly that nothing is clear in this world. Only fools and charlatans know and understand everything.

To Suvorin, who had also criticized the story's apparent inconclusiveness (his letter has not survived), Chekhov wrote:

The artist is not meant to be a judge of his characters and what they say; his only job is to be an impartial witness. I heard two Russians in a muddled conversation about pessimism, a conversation that solved nothing; all I am bound to do is reproduce that conversation exactly as I heard it. Drawing conclusions is up to the jury, that is, the readers. My only job is to be talented, that is, to know how to distinguish important testimony from unimportant, to place my characters in the proper light and speak their language.

These modest and sensible disclaimers—which have been much quoted and are of a piece with what we know of Chekhov's attractive unpretentiousness—cannot be taken at face value, of course. Chekhov understood his characters very well (he invented them, after all), and his stories are hardly deadpan journalistic narratives. But his pose of journalistic uninquisitiveness is no mere writer's waffle produced to ward off unwelcome discussion. It refers to something that is actually present in the work, to a kind of bark of the prosaic in which Chekhov consistently encases a story's vital poetic core, as if such protection were necessary for its survival. The stories have a straightforward, natural, rational, modern surface; they have been described as modest, delicate, gray. In fact they are wild and strange, archaic and brilliantly painted. But the wildness and strangeness and archaism and brilliant colors are concealed, as are the complexity and difficulty. "Everything you write is so appetizing and real that it can be easily and pleasantly swallowed." We swallow a Chekhov story as if it were an ice, and we cannot account for our feeling of repletion.

To be sure, all works of literary realism practice a kind of benevolent deception, lulling us into the state we enter at night when we mistake the fantastic productions of our imagination for actual events. But Chekhov succeeds so well in rendering his illusion of realism and in hiding the traces of his surrealism that he remains the most misunderstood— as well as the most beloved—of the nineteenth-century Russian geniuses. In Russia, no less than in our country, possibly even more than in our country, Chekhov attracts a kind of sickening piety. You utter the name "Chekhov" and people arrange their features as if a baby deer had come into the room. "Ah, Chekhov!" my guide in Moscow—a plump, blond, heavily made-up woman named Sonia—had exclaimed. "He is not a Russian writer. He is a writer for all humanity!" Chekhov would have relished Sonia. He might have—in fact he had—used her as a character. She was a dead ringer for Natasha, the crass sister-in-law in *Three Sisters,* who pushes her way into control of the Prozorov household and pushes out the three delicate, refined sisters. Sonia saw her job as guide as an exercise in control, and over the two days I spent with her I grew to detest her—

though never in the serious way one comes to detest Natasha. My struggle with Sonia was almost always over small-stakes points of touristic arrangement; and her power to get to me was, of course, further blunted by my journalist's wicked awareness of the incalculable journalistic value of poor character. After delivering herself of her estimate of Chekhov, Sonia went on to speak of unpleasant experiences she had had with certain previous American clients who had put her down. "They considered themselves superior to me," she said, but when I asked her how they had shown this she couldn't say. "I just felt it." Then she added (as I somehow knew she would) that it was never the rich Americans who made her feel inferior, always the other kind.

One of my major battles with Sonia was over the issue of a two-hour visit to the Armory in the Kremlin, scheduled for the next day and, in Sonia's view, the high point of my—of every—trip to Russia. I asked Sonia what was in the Armory, and when she told me that it was a "magnificent" collection of armor and ancient gold and gems and Fabergé eggs, I said that that kind of thing didn't interest me, and that I would just as soon skip it. Sonia looked at me as if I had gone mad. Then she abruptly said that skipping the Armory was impossible: the tour was scheduled, and it was too late to change the schedule. I repeated that I would prefer not to go to the Armory, and Sonia lapsed into silence. We were in a car, on our way to Melikhovo, Chekhov's country house, forty miles south of Moscow. Sonia began to converse in Russian with Vladimir, the driver, and continued doing so for many miles. In St. Petersburg, when Nelly spoke to our driver, Sergei—usually to give him some direction—she did so tersely and apologetically. Sonia used her talk with the driver as a form of punishment. Finally, she turned to me and said, "It is essential that you see the Armory—even for only forty-five minutes." "All right," I said. But Sonia was not satisfied. My attitude was so clearly wrong. "Tell me something," Sonia said. "When you were in St. Petersburg, did you go to the Hermitage?" "Yes," I said. "Well," Sonia said in a tone of triumph, "the Armory is much more important than the Hermitage."

When we arrived at Melikhovo, I recognized the house from pictures I had seen, but was surprised by the grounds, which were a disorderly spread of wild vegetation, haphazardly placed trees, and untended flower beds. There seemed to be no plan; the grounds made no sense as the setting for a house. Chekhov bought Melikhovo in the winter of 1892 and moved there with his parents, his sister, and his younger brothers, Ivan and Michael, in the spring. It was a small, run-down estate, which Chekhov rapidly transformed: the uncomfortable house was made snug and agreeable, kitchen and flower gardens were put in, an orchard was planted, a pond dug, the surrounding fields planted with rye and clover and oats. It was characteristic of Chekhov to make things work; thirteen years earlier he had arrived in Moscow, to start medical school, and pulled his family out of poverty by what seems like sheer force of character. The father's store had failed and he had fled to Moscow to escape debtor's prison. Alexander and the second-oldest brother, Nikolai, were already in Moscow studying at the university, and the mother and sister and younger brothers followed; sixteen-year-old Anton was left behind in Taganrog to finish high school. Little is known about the three years Chekhov spent alone in Taganrog. He boarded with the man who had, like Lopakhin in *The Cherry Orchard,* bailed out the family at a crucial moment, for the price of their home. Anton was not a brilliant student, but he graduated and received a scholarship from the town for his further studies. He was a tall, robust boy with a large head, a genial nature, and a gift for comedy. (He had entertained his family and now entertained his classmates with imitations and skits.)

When Chekhov rejoined his family in Moscow, in 1880, the possessor of what the critic James Wood has called a "strange, sourceless maturity," he quickly became its head. The authoritarian father, now a pitiable failure, had allowed the family to sink into disorderly destitution. The elder brothers made contributions—Alexander through writing sketches for humor magazines and Nikolai through magazine illustrations—but they lived dissolute lives, and only when Anton, too, began writing humorous sketches did the family's fortunes change. He wrote strictly for money; if some other way of making money had come to hand, he would have taken it. The humor writing was wretchedly paid, but Chekhov wrote so quickly and easily and unceasingly that he was able to bring in considerable income. In the early writings, no hint of the author of "The Duel" or "The Lady with the Dog" is to be found. Most of the sketches were broadly humorous, like pieces in college humor magazines, and if some are less juvenile than others, and a few make one smile, none of them are distinguished. Chekhov began to show signs of becoming Chekhov only when he turned his hand to writing short fiction that wasn't funny. By 1886, his writing was attracting serious critical attention as well as bringing in real money. Because of Chekhov's earnings from his writings (he never made any money as a physician; he mostly treated peasants, free), the family was able to move to progressively better quarters in Moscow. The purchase of Melikhovo was a culminating product of Chekhov's literary success—and of the illusion (one that Russian writers, Chekhov included, are particularly good at mocking) that life in the country is a solution to the problem of living.

With his characteristic energy and dispatch, Chekhov organized his family so that there was a productive division of labor—the mother cooked, the sister took care of the kitchen garden, Ivan did the agriculture, and Anton took charge of horticulture, for which he proved to have great talent. (The father, who had been and remained a religious fanatic, would retreat to his room for his observances and the making of herbal remedies.) Chekhov came remarkably close to living out the pastoral ideal, and even passed the test that city people who moved to the country in nineteenth-century Russia invariably, ingloriously flunked—that of being helpful to the peasants. Chekhov built three schools, donated his services as a doctor, and worked in famine and cholera relief—all the while writing some of his best stories, and almost never being without a houseful of visitors. (His frequent, abrupt removals to Moscow or St. Petersburg suggest that the problem of living remained.)

Although I recognized the house, I was actually seeing not the one in the photographs—which had been torn down in the 1920s—but a replica, built in the late '40s. (Resurrecting destroyed buildings seems to be a national tic. In Moscow I saw a huge church with gold domes that was a recently completed replica of one of the churches Stalin wantonly tore down.) The interiors of Melikhovo had been carefully restored, re-created from photographs supplied by Maria Chekhova, then in her eighties. The rooms were small and appealingly furnished; they gave a sense of a pleasant, very well-run home. The walls were covered with Morris-print-like wallpapers, and over them paintings and family photographs hung in dense arrangements. Everything was simple, handsome, unaffected. But I think that Chekhov would have found it absurd. The idea of rebuilding his house from scratch would have offended his sense of the fitness of things. I can imagine him walking through the rooms with a look of irony on his face as he listened to the prepared speech of our tour guide, Ludmilla. Ludmilla was a youngish woman with glasses, dressed in trousers and a shabby maroon snow jacket, who was full of knowledge of Chekhov's life but had read little of his work. She spoke of Chekhov with a radiant expression on her face. She told me (through Sonia) that a good deal of the furniture and many objects in the house were original; when the house was being torn down the local peasants had sacked it, but during the restoration returned much of what they had taken. I asked if they had been forced to do so by the Soviet authorities, and she said, "Oh, no. They did so gladly. Everyone loved Anton Pavlovich." When I questioned her about how she came to be working at the museum she gave a long reply: She had never been able to read Chekhov; his writing left her cold. But one day she visited Melikhovo (she lived in a nearby town) and while in the house had had some sort of incredible spiritual experience, which she cannot explain. She kept returning to Melikhovo—it drew her like a magnet—and finally the director of the museum had given her a job.

After finishing her tour of the ersatz house and the disorderly garden, Ludmilla walked out to the exit with Sonia and me, and from her answer to one of my questions it appeared that she wasn't paid for her work. "So you work here as a volunteer," I said. "No," she said, she just wasn't paid, the way many people in Russia were not being paid now. Wages were frequently "delayed" for months, even years. I asked Ludmilla how she lived if she wasn't paid. Did she have another job that did pay? Sonia—not relaying my question—looked at me angrily and said, "We will not talk about this. This is not your subject. We will talk about Chekhov."

I debated with myself whether to challenge Sonia, and decided I would. I said, "Look, if we're going to talk about Chekhov, we need to say that Anton Pavlovich cared about truth above all else. He did not look away from reality. People not being paid for work is something he would have talked about—not brushed away with 'Let's talk about Chekhov.'" I sounded a little ridiculous to myself—like someone doing an imitation of a character in a socialist realist novel—but I enjoyed Sonia's discomposure, and when she started to answer I cut her off with "Tell Ludmilla what I just said." Sonia obeyed, and Ludmilla, smiling her sweet smile, said, "This is why I find it hard to read Chekhov. There is too much sadness in it. It is his spirituality that attracts me—the spirituality I receive from learning about his life."

On the drive back to Moscow, Sonia praised the "good

taste" of Melikhovo, before relapsing into conversation with Vladimir. He was a large, swarthy man of around fifty, wearing a black leather coat and exuding a New York taxi driver's gruff savoir faire. The contrast between him and Sergei, my St. Petersburg driver, a slender young man who dressed in jeans and carried a book, was like the contrast between Moscow and St. Petersburg themselves. St. Petersburg was small and faded and elegant and a little unreal; Moscow was big and unlovely and the real thing in a city. St. Petersburg came at you sideways; Moscow immediately delivered the message of its scale and power. Chekhov loved Moscow and had reserved feelings about St. Petersburg, even though his literary career got properly under way only when, in 1882, the St. Petersburg editor and publisher A. N. Leiken invited him to write for his humorous weekly, *Fragments,* and moved into full gear when he began writing for Suvorin's St. Petersburg daily *New Times.* He would visit St. Petersburg, first to see Leiken and then Suvorin, but he never really warmed to the city. In his fiction, people from St. Petersburg tend to be suspect (In "An Anonymous Story" an unsympathetic character named Orlov is described as a St. Petersburg dandy) or apologetic ("I was born in cold, idle Petersburg," the sympathetic Tuzenbach says in *Three Sisters*). In St. Petersburg, Chekhov suffered the worst literary failure of his life, with *The Seagull*—comparable to Henry James's failure with *Guy Domville.* At its premiere, at the Alexandrinsky Theater in 1896, it was booed and jeered, and the reviews were savage. (According to Simmons, "The *News* dismissed the play as 'entirely absurd' from every point of view," and a reviewer for the *Bourse News* said the play was "not *The Seagull* but simply a wild fowl.") The failure is generally attributed to a special circumstance of the premiere: it was a benefit for a beloved comic actress named E. I. Levkeeva, and so the audience was largely made up of Levkeeva fans, who expected hilarity and, to their disbelief and growing outrage, got Symbolism. At its next performance, which was attended by a normal Petersburg audience, *The Seagull* was calmly and appreciatively received, and positive criticism began to appear in the newspapers. But by that time Chekhov had crawled back to Melikhovo, and believed that he was finished as a playwright. "Never again will I write plays or have them staged," he wrote to Suvorin.

Because of Chekhov's slender and ambivalent ties to St. Petersburg, the city has no Chekhov museum, but a few of his letters and manuscripts have strayed into its Pushkin Museum, and on the morning of my first day in Nelly's charge she took me to inspect them. We sat at a table covered with dark green cloth, opposite a young, round-faced archivist named Tatyana, who displayed each document like a jeweler displaying a costly necklace or brooch. (Once, when Nelly reached out her hand toward a document,

Tatyana playfully slapped it.) Chekhov's small, spidery handwriting, very delicate and light, brought to mind Tolstoy's description of him as reported by Maxim Gorky: "What a dear, beautiful man; he is modest and quiet like a girl. And he walks like a girl." One of Tatyana's exhibits was a letter of 1887 to the writer Dmitri Grigorovich, commenting on a story of Grigorovich's called "Karelin's Dream." Today, Grigorovich's work is no longer read; his name figures in literary history largely because of a fan letter he wrote to Chekhov in March 1886. At the time, Grigorovich was sixty-four and one of the major literary celebrities of the day. He wrote to tell the twenty-six-year-old Chekhov that "you have *real* talent—a talent which places you in the front rank among writers in the new generation." Grigorovich went on to counsel Chekhov to slow down, to stop writing so much, to save himself for large, serious literary effort. "Cease to write hurriedly. I do not know what your financial situation is. If it is poor, it would be better for you to go hungry, as we did in our day, and save your impressions for a mature, finished work, written not in one sitting, but during the happy hours of inspiration." Chekhov wrote back:

> Your letter, my kind, warmly beloved herald of glad tidings, struck me like a thunderbolt. I nearly wept, I was profoundly moved, and even now I feel that it has

left a deep imprint on my soul. . . . I, indeed, can find neither words nor actions to show my gratitude. You know with what eyes ordinary people look upon such outstanding people like yourself, hence you may realize what your letter means for my self-esteem. . . . I am as in a daze. I lack the ability to judge whether or not I merit this great reward.

Chekhov went on to acknowledge the haste and carelessness with which he wrote:

I don't recall a *single* tale of mine over which I have worked more than a day, and "The Hunter," which pleased you, I wrote in the bathhouse! I have written my stories the way reporters write up their notes about fires—mechanically, half-consciously, caring nothing about either the reader or myself.

And:

What first drove me to take a critical view of my writing was . . . a letter from Suvorin. I began to think of writing some purposeful piece, but nevertheless I did not have faith in my own literary direction.

And now, all of a sudden, your letter arrived. You must forgive the comparison, but it had the same effect on me as a government order "to get out of the city in twenty-four hours." That is, I suddenly felt the need for haste, to get out of this rut, where I am stuck, as quickly as possible.

In his letter about "Karelin's Dream," Chekhov gives a remarkable account of the way being cold at night gets into one's dreams:

When at night the quilt falls off I begin to dream of huge slippery stones, of cold autumnal water, naked banks—and all this dim, misty, without a patch of blue sky; sad and dejected like one who has lost his way, I look at the stones and feel that for some reason I cannot avoid crossing a deep river; I see then small tugs that drag huge barges, floating beams. All this is infinitely grey, damp, and dismal. When I run from the river I come across the fallen cemetery gates, funerals, my school teachers. . . . And all the time I am cold through and through with that oppressive nightmare-like cold which is impossible in walking life, and which is only felt by those who are asleep. . . . When I feel cold I always dream of my teacher of scripture, a learned priest of imposing appearance, who insulted my mother when I was a little boy; I dream of vindictive, implacable, intriguing people, smiling with spiteful glee—such as one can never see in waking life. The laughter at the carriage window is a characteristic symptom of Karelin's nightmare. When in dreams one feels the presence of some evil will, the inevitable ruin brought about by some outside force, one always hears something like such laughter. . . .

These dreams, in their atmosphere of dread and uncanniness, put one in mind of the novels of Dostoevsky and the paintings of Edvard Munch, and hint at anxieties of which Chekhov preferred never to speak. Chekhov's biographers regularly note his reserve, even as they attempt to break it down. With the opening of the Soviet archives, hitherto unknown details of Chekhov's love life and sex life have emerged. But the value of this new information—much of it derived from passages or phrases cut out of Chekhov's published letters by the puritanical Soviet censorship, and absurdly said to make him "more human"—is questionable. That Chekhov was not prudish about or uninterested in sex is hardly revealed by his use of a coarse word in a letter; it is implicit in the stories and plays. Chekhov would be unperturbed, and probably even amused, by the stir the restored cuts have created—as if the documentary proof of sexual escapades or of incidents of impotence disclosed anything essential about him, anything that crosses the boundary between his inner and outer life. Chekhov's privacy is safe from the biographer's attempts upon it—as, indeed, are all privacies, even those of the most apparently open and even exhibitionistic natures. The letters and journals we leave behind and the impressions we have made on our contemporaries are the mere husk of the kernel of our essential life. When we die, the kernel is buried with us. This is the horror and pity of death and the reason for the inescapable triviality of biography.

The attentive reader of Chekhov will notice a piece of plagiarism I have just committed. The image of the kernel and the husk comes from another famous passage in "The Lady with the Dog," in the story's last section. Gurov, after parting with Anna at the end of the summer and returning to his loveless marriage in Moscow, finds that he can't get her out of his mind, travels to the provincial town where she lives with the husband *she* doesn't love, and is now clandestinely meeting with her in a hotel in Moscow, to which she comes every month or so, telling her husband she is seeing a specialist. One snowy morning, on his way to the hotel, Gurov reflects on his situation (all the while conversing with his daughter, whom he will drop off at school before proceeding to his tryst):

> He had two lives: one, open, seen and known by all who cared to know, full of relative truth and of relative falsehood, exactly like the lives of his friends and acquaintances; and another life running its course in secret. And through some strange, perhaps accidental, conjunction of circumstances, everything that was es-

sential, of interest and of value to him, everything that
made the kernel of his life, was hidden from other people; and all that was false in him, the sheath in which
he hid himself to conceal the truth—such, for instance,
as his work in the bank, his discussions at the club . . .
his presence with his wife at anniversary festivities—all
that was open. And he judged of others by himself, not
believing in what he saw, and always believing that
every man had his real, most interesting life under the
cover of secrecy and under the cover of night. All personal life rested on secrecy, and possibly it was partly
on that account that civilized man was so nervously
anxious that personal privacy should be respected.

"The Lady with the Dog" is said to be Chekhov's riposte
to *Anna Karenina,* his defense of illicit love against Tolstoy's harsh (if ambivalent) condemnation of it. But
Chekhov's *Anna* (if this is what it is) bears no real resem-
blance to Tolstoy's; comparing the two only draws attention
to the differences between Chekhov's realism and Tolstoy's.
Gurov is no Vronsky, and Anna von Diderits is no Anna
Karenina. Neither of the Chekhov characters has the partic-
ularity, the vivid lifelikeness of the Tolstoy lovers. They are
indistinct, more like figures in an allegory than like characters in a novel. Nor is Chekhov concerned, as Tolstoy is,
with adultery as a social phenomenon. In *Anna Karenina,*

the lovers occupy only a section of a crowded canvas; in "The Lady with the Dog," the lovers fill the canvas. Other people appear in the story—the crowd at the Yalta harbor, a Moscow official with whom Gurov plays cards, the daughter he walks to school, a couple of servants—but they are shadowy figures, without names. (Even the dog is unnamed—when Gurov arrives at Anna's house, and sees a servant walking it, Chekhov makes a point of noting that "in his excitement he could not remember the dog's name.") The story has a close, hermetic atmosphere. No one knows of the affair, or suspects its existence. It is as if it were taking place in a sealed box made of dark glass that the lovers can see out of, but no one can see into. The story enacts what the passage about Gurov's double life states. It can be read as an allegory of interiority. The beauty of Gurov and Anna's secret love—and of interior life—is precisely its hiddenness. Chekhov often said that he hated lies more than anything. "The Lady with the Dog" plays with the paradox that a lie—a husband deceiving a wife or a wife deceiving a husband—can be the fulcrum of truth of feeling, a vehicle of authenticity. (Tolstoy would argue that this is the kind of self-deception adulterers classically indulge in, and that a lie is a lie.) But the story's most interesting and complicated paradox lies in the inversion of the inner-outer formula by which imaginative literature is perforce propelled. Even as Gurov hugs his secret to himself, we know all about it. If privacy is life's most precious possession, it is fiction's least considered one. A fictional character is a being who has no privacy, who stands before the reader with his "real, most interesting life" nakedly exposed. We never see people in life as clearly as we see the people in novels, stories, and plays; there is a veil between ourselves and even our closest intimates, blurring us to each other. By intimacy we mean something much more modest than the glaring exposure to which the souls of fictional characters are regularly held up. We know things about Gurov and Anna—especially about Gurov, since the story is told from his point of view—that they don't know about each other, and feel no discomfort in our voyeurism. We consider it our due as readers. It does not occur to us that the privacy rights we are so nervously anxious to safeguard for ourselves should be extended to fictional characters. But, interestingly, it does seem to occur to Chekhov. If he cannot draw the mantle of reticence over his characters that he draws over himself—and still call himself a fiction writer—he can stop short of fully exercising his fiction writer's privilege of omniscience. He can hold back, he can leave his characters a little blurred, their motives a little mysterious. It is this reticence that Shcheglov and Suvorin were responding to in their criticism of "Lights." Chekhov's replies, with their appealing expressions of epistemological humility and journalistic detachment, skirt the issue, put his interlocutors off the scent of his characters' secrets.

In a story called "Difficult People," written in 1886, we can see the shoot from which Gurov's meditation on double life is to grow. A dreadful row has taken place at a provincial family dinner table between an authoritarian father and a rebellious son. The son storms out of the house and, full of bitterness and hatred, sets out for Moscow on foot. Then:

> "Look out!" He heard behind him a loud voice.
>
> An old lady of his acquaintance, a landowner of the neighborhood, drove past him in a light, elegant landau. He bowed to her, and smiled all over his face. And at once he caught himself in that smile, which was so out of keeping with his gloomy mood. Where did it come from if his whole heart was full of vexation and misery? And he thought nature itself had given man this capacity for lying, that even in difficult moments of spiritual strain he might be able to hide the secrets of his nest as the fox and the wild duck do. Every family has its joys and its horrors, but however great they may be, it's hard for an outsider's eye to see them; they are a secret.

Chekhov hid the secrets of his literary nest as well as those of his personal one; he was closemouthed about his compositional methods and destroyed most of his drafts. But he didn't merely withhold information *about* his literary practice; the practice itself was a kind of exercise in withholding. In his letter of March 1886 to Grigorovich, Chekhov noted a curious habit he had of doing everything he could not to "waste" on any story "the images and scenes dear to me which—God knows why—I have treasured and kept carefully hidden," and, again, writing to Suvorin in October 1888, he cited "the images which seem best to me, which I love and jealously guard, lest I spend and spoil them, adding, "All that I now write displeases and bores me, but what sits in my head interests, excites, and moves me."

In the much-anthologized story "The Kiss" (1887) Chekhov gave brilliant form to his sense of the danger of dislodging what sits in one's head from its place of safety. A brigade on the march spends the night in a provincial town, and its nineteen officers are invited for evening tea at the house of the local squire, a retired lieutenant-general named von Rabbek. The central consciousness of the story is Ryabovitch, "a little officer in spectacles, with sloping shoulders, and whiskers like a lynx's," who thinks of himself as "the shyest, most modest, and most undistinguished officer in the whole brigade." At von Rabbek's house Ryabovitch is struck by the social adroitness of the host and hostess and their grown son and daughter, who have invited the officers strictly out of duty, and at a time when it is inconvenient to do so—they are having a house party—but who put on a dazzling performance of hospitality. "Von

Rabbek and his family skillfully drew the officers into the discussion, and meanwhile kept a sharp lookout over their glasses and mouths, to see whether all of them were drinking, whether all had enough sugar, why someone was not eating cakes or not drinking brandy. And the longer Ryabovitch watched and listened, the more he was attracted by this insincere but splendidly disciplined family." During a period of dancing, in which Ryabovitch does not participate ("He had never once danced in his whole life, and he had never once in his life put his arm round the waist of a respectable woman"), he follows the von Rabbek son and some officers to a billiard room in another part of the house, and then, feeling himself in the way (he does not play billiards, either), decides to return to the drawing room. But in retracing his steps Ryabovitch makes a wrong turn and finds himself in a small dark room. Suddenly, a young woman rushes toward him, murmurs "At last!" and kisses him. Realizing her mistake—she had come to the room for a lovers' tryst, clearly—she shrieks and runs off. The encounter has a momentous effect on Ryabovitch. It is almost like a conversion experience. "Something strange was happening to him. . . . His neck, round which soft, fragrant arms had so lately been clasped, seemed to him to be anointed with oil; on his left cheek near his moustache where the unknown had kissed him there was a faint chilly tingling sensation as from peppermint drops. . . . He was full of a strange new feeling which grew stronger and stronger. . . . He quite forgot that he was round-shouldered and uninteresting, that he had lynx-like whiskers and an 'undistinguished appearance.' " (That was how his appearance had been described by some ladies whose conversation he had accidentally overheard.) The next morning, the brigade leaves the town, and throughout the day's march Ryabovitch remains under the spell of the kiss, which has acted on his imagination like a powerful drug, releasing delicious fantasies of romantic love. At the end of the day, in the tent after supper, he feels the need to tell his comrades about his adventure.

> He began describing very minutely the incident of the kiss, and a moment later relapsed into silence. . . . In the course of that moment he had told everything, and it surprised him dreadfully to find how short a time it took him to tell it. He had imagined that he could have been telling the story of the kiss till next morning.

One of the officers, a sleazy womanizer named Lobytko, is moved to respond with a crude story about a sexual encounter in a train. Ryabovitch vows "never to confide again." Twelve years later, Chekhov will write another version of this scene in "The Lady with the Dog." After Gurov returns home from Yalta, he is "tormented by an intense desire to confide his memories to someone," and one evening, as he is leaving a Moscow club, he impulsively says to an official with whom he has been playing cards:

> "If only you knew what a fascinating woman I made the acquaintance of in Yalta!"
>
> The official got into his sledge and was driving away, but turned suddenly and shouted:
>
> "Dmitri Dmitrich!"
>
> "What?
>
> "You were right this evening: the sturgeon was a bit too strong!"

In both cases, something lovely and precious has been defiled by the vulgar gaze of the outer world. Both men immediately regret their impulse to confide. But the telling scene in "The Kiss" has an additional moral—a literary one. Ryabovitch makes the painful discovery that every novice writer makes about the gap that lies between thinking and writing. ("It surprised him dreadfully to find how short a time it took him to tell it.") The gossamer images that sit in one's head have to be transformed into some more durable material—that of artful narration—if they are not to dissolve into nothing when they hit the chilly outer air. Chekhov lodges the cautionary incident of Ryabovitch's artless blurting out within his own artful narration. What poor Ryabovitch fails to communicate to his comrades in his amateur's innocence Chekhov succeeds in communicating to us with his professional's guile. He is like the practiced von Rabbeks, who perform their function of giving pleasure because they must and because they know how. "You can do nothing by wisdom and holiness if God has not given you the gift," a monk in "On Easter Eve" (1886) says in a discussion of the poetics of certain hymns of praise in the Russian Orthodox liturgy called *akathistoi.* "Everything must be harmonious, brief and complete. . . . Every line must be beautified in every way; there must be flowers and lightning and wind and sun and all the objects of the visible world." Chekhov's own literary enterprise could hardly be better described. His stories and plays—even the darkest among them—are hymns of praise. Flowers and lightning and wind and sun and all the objects of the visible world appear in them as they appear in the work of no other writer. In almost every Chekhov work there is a moment when we suddenly feel as Ryabovitch felt when the young woman entered the room and kissed him.

Three

In Chekhov's garden at the villa in Autka (now called the Chekhov House Museum in Yalta), Nina had pointed out a birch tree that, she said, Chekhov himself had planted. (According to a brochure, more than half the trees and shrubs and vines in the garden, representing 149 species, were planted by Chekhov.) The garden had reached a majestic maturity Chekhov did not live to see—indeed, would not have lived to see had he had a normal life span. It is a hundred years since the garden was laid out, on a bare, dry piece of land near a Tatar cemetery. In May, it had a delicious fragrant lushness. Shrubs and flowers spilled out over paths leading through a kind of maze of variegated green shadiness.

The conventional literary association of gardens with love and youth and renewal is a touchstone of Chekhov's art. In his stories and plays, gardens are pervasive, almost insistent, presences. Courtships are regularly conducted in them—in the way (as Robert Alter points out in *The Art of*

Biblical Narrative) that betrothals in the Hebrew Scriptures regularly result from encounters at wells. (Gurov and Anna first meet in a restaurant set in a garden.) Intimations of happiness gleam from them. Nothing bad can happen in a garden—except possibly the melancholy induced by the ending of a long summer afternoon. Bad things can happen *to* a garden, of course. The most famous example is the chopping down of the trees at the end of *The Cherry Orchard*. In a less well known work, the story "The Black Monk" (1894), another great garden is lost, this one through the miscalculation of its owner, an old horticulturist named Yegor Pesotsky. In an attempt to secure his garden's survival after his death, Pesotsky marries off his daughter to precisely the man most likely to hasten its ruin—a deranged student of philosophy named Kovrin, who believes that he is one of "the chosen of God," destined to lead mankind into "the kingdom of eternal truth." (His lunacy takes the form of a chronic hallucination in which a monk dressed in black emerges from a whirlwind and eggs him on in his grandiosity.) In contrast, Pesotsky is a model of sanity, a kind of horticultural William Morris. "Look at me," he says, "I do everything myself. I work from morning to night: I do all the grafting myself, the pruning myself, the planting myself. . . . The whole secret lies in loving it—that is, in the sharp eye of the master; yes, and in the master's hands, and in the feeling that makes one, when one goes anywhere for an hour's visit,

sit ill at ease, with one's heart far way, afraid that something may have happened to the garden." The worst thing that can happen to a garden, he tells Kovrin, "is not a hare, not a cockchafer, and not the frost but any outside person"—the stranger who will come along after his death. Like long summer afternoons, gardens are ephemeral. The old man's attempt to give his garden immortality proves to be as vain as Kovrin's megalomaniacal quest for eternal truth. And yet here at Autka was Chekhov's garden intact, and more beautiful with every passing year! Outside persons had not destroyed it but were tenderly caring for it—as if in fulfillment of Chekhov's prophecy (one that he liked to put into the mouths of certain of his weak, appealing characters) that human nature would improve in the future.

In *Three Sisters,* Vershinin says to Masha, Irina, and Olga:

> When a little more time has passed—another two or three hundred years—people will look at our present manner of life with horror and derision, and everything of today will seem awkward and heavy, and very strange and uncomfortable. Oh, what a wonderful life that will be—what a wonderful life! . . . There are only three of your sort in the town now, but in generations to come there will be more and more and more; and the time will come when everything will be changed and be as you would have it; they will live in your way,

and later on you too will be out of date—people will be born who will be better than you. . . ."

And Astrov in *Uncle Vanya:*

> Those who will live a hundred or two hundred years after us, and who will despise us for having lived our lives so stupidly and tastelessly—they will, perhaps, find a means of being happy. . . .

Astrov is also—and chiefly—known for his concern about the destruction of the Russian forests and for his remarkable grasp of the principles of ecology, decades before the term came into use as we now know it. A. P. Chudakov and Simon Karlinsky have both written of Chekhov as a kind of protoenvironmentalist. "In the twentieth century the preservation of nature has long been and will be more and more the measure by which the moral potential of each person is tested," Chudakov writes in *Chekhov's Poetics* (1971; published in English in 1983). "[Chekhov] was the first in literature who included the relationship of man to nature in his sphere of ethics." Karlinsky, in the introduction to his invaluable *Anton Chekhov's Life and Thought: Selected Letters and Commentary* (1973), and in an essay entitled "Huntsmen, Birds, Forests and Three Sisters" (1981), writes of Chekhov's prescient uneasiness about the destruction of ecosystems. In the essay, Karlinsky speculates about the literary and scientific sources of Chekhov's environmentalism, citing Thoreau, James Fenimore Cooper, the French geographer Elisée Reclus, and the Russian climatologist Alexander Voyeykov. But writing of the nature symbolism in *Three Sisters,* he makes a telling error:

> At the end of the play, Natasha intends to consolidate her victory by chopping down the beautiful trees. . . . "I will order them first of all to chop down this avenue of firs, and then this maple tree here. . . . It is so ugly in the evening." After destroying the magnificent trees that meant so much to the departing Vershinin and the exterminated Tuzenbach, Natasha plans to replace free nature with a tame variant of it that is acceptable to her: "And here I will order them to plant little flowers, lots of little flowers, and they'll smell. . . ."

Avenues of firs and specimen maples are, of course, no more a part of "free nature" than are beds of tacky little flowers. They belong to what Michael Pollan has wonderfully called "second nature"—the sphere of horticulture. In his writings, as in his life, Chekhov was a good deal less involved with trees growing in the forest than with those planted in an orchard. He was a poet of the domesticated landscape rather than of the Sublime, drawn more to the charm of a shady old garden than to the grandiloquence of untouched wilderness. In the story "Ariadne" (1895), a character named Lubkov "would sometimes stand still before some magnificent landscape and say: 'It would be nice to have tea here.'"

Lubkov is an unsympathetic figure, and Chekhov is mocking him; but it is not unlikely that he is satirizing himself as well.

Chekhov hated theatricality and was evidently as uncomfortable with nature's histrionics as with man's. In "The Duel" (1891), he employs a dramatic Caucasian landscape of craggy mountains and steep gorges to objectify the Romantic posturings of his hero, Ivan Andreitch Laevsky, the most fully developed of his redeemable cads. Before Laevsky can undergo his transformation from a hysterically miserable man who hasn't fully grown up into an ordinarily unhappy adult, he must be brought low. He must come down from the high places of Byronic self-involvement to the sea level of Chekhovian compassion. ("The Duel" could be described as a *Hamlet* that turns into a *Lear.*) Laevsky has run off to the Caucasus with a young married woman named Nadezhda Fyodorovna, of whom he has predictably tired and whom he callously plans to abandon. Laevsky's adversary, Nicholas von Koren, is a rigidly upright young scientist who believes that people like Laevsky ought to be eliminated, and who puts his chilly philosophy into effect by almost killing Laevsky in a duel. However, it is not von Koren who teaches Laevsky the transformative lesson, but Nadezhda. She is one of Chekhov's most striking and subtle portraits of women. Like Anna Sergeyevna—like all the women who fall in love with Chekhov's flawed heroes—she is a rather pathetic figure. Chekhov does not condemn married women who take up with men like Gurov and Laevsky, but he has no illusions about what they have let themselves in for. ("It was clear to both of them that they had still a long, long road before them, and that the most complicated and difficult part of it was only just beginning," he writes of Anna and Gurov at the end of his story but not of theirs.) Unlike the delicate, almost virginal Anna, the assertive, plumply pretty Nadezhda has sex on her mind all the time:

> The long, insufferably hot, wearisome days, beautiful languorous evenings and stifling nights, and the whole manner of living, when from morning to night one is at a loss to fill up the useless hours, and the persistent thought that she was the prettiest young woman in the town, and that her youth was passing and being wasted, and Laevsky himself, though honest and idealistic, always the same, always lounging about in his slippers, biting his nails, and wearing her out with his caprices, led by degrees to her becoming possessed by desire, and as though she were mad, she thought of nothing else night and day. Breathing, looking, walking, she felt nothing but desire. The sound of the sea told her she must love; the darkness of evening said the same; the mountains the same. . . .

At a picnic among the craggy mountains and steep gorges, Nadezhda "wanted to skip and jump, to laugh, to shout, to tease, to flirt. In her cheap cotton dress with blue pansies on it, in her red shoes and . . . straw hat, she seemed to herself, little, simple, light, ethereal as a butterfly." She cavorts among the rocks with two of the men at the picnic. Later, she realizes "she had gone too far, had been too free and easy in her behavior, and, overcome with misery, feeling herself heavy, stout, coarse, and drunk, she got into the first empty carriage."

Chekhov has been called a misogynist, but in the face of such an acutely sensitive and sympathetic portrait as that of Nadezhda, the characterization does not hold up. "The Duel," as its title suggests, is about the struggle between the ideologies and temperaments represented by Laevsky and von Koren and is apparently a work about men; but its driving force is what can only be called a kind of feminism. The fulcrum of Laevsky's transformation is his realization that Nadezhda is a human being like him. He has found her in bed with one of the men she flirted with at the picnic, having been led to the place of assignation by the other:

> He was in an insufferable anguish of loathing and misery. Kirilin and Atchmianov were loathsome, but they were only continuing what he had begun; they were his accomplices and his disciples. This young, weak woman had trusted him more than a brother, and he had deprived her of her husband, of her friends and of her country, and had brought her here—to the heat, to fever, and to boredom; and from day to day she was

bound to reflect, like a mirror, his idleness, his vicious-
ness and falsity—and that was all she had had to fill
her weak, listless, pitiable life.

Laevsky has these thoughts sitting at a table in his house on
the eve of the duel. A storm rages outside, and he remembers

how as a boy he used to run out into the garden without a hat on when there was a storm, and how two
fair-haired girls with blue eyes used to run after him,
and how they got wet through with the rain; they
laughed with delight, but when there was a loud peal
of thunder, the girls used to nestle up to the boy con-
fidingly, while he crossed himself and made haste to
repeat: "Holy, holy, holy. . . ." Oh, where had they
vanished to! In what sea were they drowned, those
dawning days of pure, fair life? He had no fear of the
storm, no love of nature now; he had no God. All the
confiding girls he had ever known had by now been
ruined by him and those like him. All his life he had
not planted one tree in his own garden, nor grown one
blade of grass; and living among the living, he had not
saved one fly; he had done nothing but destroy and
ruin, and lie, lie. . . .

After the storm is over, a scene takes place between
Nadezhda and Laevsky that catches the reader unawares
and almost too violently tugs at his heart:

"How miserable I am!" she said. "If only you knew
how miserable I am! I expected," she went on, half
closing her eyes, "that you would kill me or turn me
out of the house into the rain and storm, but you
delay . . . delay. . . ."

Warmly and impulsively he put his arms around her
and covered her knees and hands with kisses . . . he
stroked her hair and looking into her face, realized that
this unhappy, sinful woman was the one creature near
and dear to him, whom no one could replace.

The duel takes place among the craggy mountains and steep
gorges—the landscape where Lermontov's Pechorin fought
his deadly duel with Grushnitskii. Lest the reader fail to
hear the Lermontovean echo, and to grasp its irony,
Chekhov inserts a farcical moment, when no one at the duel
knows exactly what to do. " 'Gentlemen, who remembers
the description in Lermontov?' asked von Koren, laugh-
ing." Laevsky escapes with his life. (He had fired in the air,
and von Koren, on the point of going through with his in-
tended execution of the useless, is distracted by a cry from a
deacon who has seen the murderous look on his face.)
Then, as a prelude to a new life of ordinary kindness and
responsibility, Laevsky and Nadezhda sit in a garden—
where else?—"huddled close together, saying nothing, or
dreaming aloud of their happy life in the future, in brief,
broken sentences, while it seemed to him that he had never

spoken at such length or so eloquently." The story ends with a glimpse of their new life, and with no assurance that they will be able to sustain the rigors of an existence stripped of illusion and devoted to prosaic work. Characteristically, Chekhov does not allow them the comfort of Tolstoyan pastoral—he does not let them fulfill the fantasy that brought them to the Caucasus. ("We would pick out a plot of ground, would toil in the sweat of our brow, would have a vineyard and a field, and so on.") The work Laevsky does to pay his debts is not horticulture but the tedious, ill-paid work of copying. (How Nadezhda spends her days is left to the reader's imagination. When we last see her, she is a recessive, diminished figure.) Chekhov's gardens at Melikhovo and Autka were his hobby; the gardens in his stories and plays, like Marianne Moore's imaginary gardens with real toads in them, are something more serious. (This may be why Chekhov never entrusted them to amateurs; his imaginary gardens are always in the care of professionals.) The garden in which Laevsky and Nadezhda huddle—like the garden of his youth, like every garden in Chekhov—is a symbolic place of grace. The garden at Autka is merely a real garden.

Four

"They say that Olga refused to sleep with Chekhov because she was afraid of catching his TB," Nina says as we walk back to the car along the footpath above the sea in Oreanda.

"I've never heard that," I say. "From their correspondence it seems clear that they *did* sleep together."

"Don't you remember at Gurzuv, when you asked about the narrow bed in Chekhov's room?"

I do remember. The day before, we had visited the seaside cottage, twelve miles outside of Yalta, that Chekhov bought soon after building his villa. One could understand why he was unable to resist it. The three-room wooden house, with a porch, sits directly on the shore of a rocky coastline rimmed by cliffs; a few stone steps to the right of the door lead straight into the water. It was now a state-run museum—like the houses in Autka and Melikhovo and the town house in Moscow where the Chekhov family lived—

and two agreeable women were in charge of it. One, named Lydia, was young and very well dressed—she wore a fashionable white suit and high heels. The other, Eva, an older woman, who turned out to have been at the university with Nina, was more plainly dressed. When we arrived they were sitting on the porch, at a table with a pitcher of wildflowers on it, looking out at the water. Lydia was designated as our guide and she took us into a room that served as an entry hall (pausing to sell us admission tickets) and exhibition space for photographs and memorabilia pertaining to *Three Sisters,* much of which Chekhov wrote in the cottage. The second, and final, room on view (the kitchen was not open for inspection) was Chekhov's reconstituted bedroom. The bed, covered with a chaste white spread, was extremely narrow, and when I wondered how he and Olga had managed to sleep in it, Lydia explained that what was now the entry hall had been Olga's bedroom. Nina, having grown up in a society where five families lived in a single room, was perhaps unaware that it was customary for pre-Revolution bourgeois married couples to sleep in separate bedrooms. But her dark comment reflected a larger negative feeling about Olga. Russians have not taken Olga to their hearts as they have Chekhov. Harvey Pitcher, the author of a sympathetic book about Olga called *Chekhov's Leading Lady* (1979), writes that the marriage of Chekhov and Olga "was the subject of a controversy that has never died down. Olga

Knipper might be recognized as the Moscow Art Theater's leading actress and interpreter of Chekhov's heroines . . . but how had she succeeded in marrying Russia's most elusive literary bachelor when he was already past forty? Could she be anything but one of those predatory females often described by Chekhov himself in his fiction? And what sort of wife was it who for more than half the year continued to pursue her acting career in Moscow while her husband was confined for health reasons to the Crimean resort of Yalta, more than two days' journey from Moscow by train?"

But the enforced separation may have been crucial to the marriage's success—perhaps even to its very being. In 1895 (three years before he met Olga) Chekhov wrote to Suvorin:

> Very well then, I shall marry if you so desire. But under the following conditions: everything must continue as it was before; in other words, she must live in Moscow and I in the country, and I'll go visit her. I will never be able to stand the sort of happiness that lasts from one day to the next, from one morning to the next. Whenever someone talks to me day after day about the same thing in the same tone of voice, it brings out the ferocity in me. . . . I promise to be a splendid husband, but give me a wife who, like the moon, does not appear in my sky every day. [In "A Dreary Story" (1889) Chekhov writes mordantly of a

wife who says exactly the same thing to her husband every morning.]

The separation had another benefit—the correspondence it generated. Biographers rue the destruction or loss of letters; they might also curse the husband and wife who never leave each other's side, and thus perform a kind of epistolary abortion. The letters between Olga and Anton—available in an English translation by Jean Benedetti in a volume entitled *Dear Writer, Dear Actress* (1996)—make wonderful reading. One marvels at the almost uncanny similarity of style between writer and actress, until one stops to remember that actors are mimics. Olga performs on paper as she performed on the stage and in life. What she does, of course—what the actors among our friends do—is only an exaggerated version of the unconscious mimicry of the other we all engage in when we are making ourselves agreeable. The correspondence permits us to trace the relationship from its beginning, as a flirtatious friendship, to the period when the two became lovers, to the marriage itself, which probably would not have occurred if Chekhov had been left to his own devices. The letters record Olga's pressings, his dodgings, and his eventual capitulation, on the condition that "you give your word that no one in Moscow will know about our marriage until it has actually happened. . . . Because I have a horror of weddings, the congratulations and

the champagne, standing around glass in hand with an endless grin on your face. . . ."

The Russians' perception of Olga as an ambitious, cold,
ruthless, unkind woman, not worthy of the gentle, delicate
Anton Pavlovich, is not borne out by her letters, which are
consistently gentle and delicate. But Olga's German background—she came from an assimilated German family, like
that of Anna Sergeyevna von Diderits's husband—may have
some bearing on the dislike and resentment she has attracted,
as may her post-Revolution career as a leading People's
Artist. (She lived until the 1950s and never stopped acting.)
In an article entitled "The Heart of Chekhov" (1959), Leo
Rabeneck—who by chance had been present when Chekhov
died in Badenweiler, and who stayed in touch with Olga until
the Revolution, when he emigrated to Paris—gives us a chilling glimpse of her life under the Soviets:

> The last time I saw Olga Leonardovna was in 1937,
> when the [Moscow] Art Theatre had come to Paris.
> After the performance I went to a small bistro where
> the actors usually dined. As I came in I saw Olga
> Leonardovna sitting at a table with two men I didn't
> know. When she saw me, she quickly looked down at
> her plate until I had passed by. I understood she
> couldn't speak to me. The next morning, I was walking
> along the Champs-Elysées, when I happened to meet
> Kachalov [the leading male actor of the Moscow Art

Theater]. We kissed and embraced. I told him how
Olga Leonardovna had pretended not to know me.

Kachalov replied: Lev L'vovich, she was sitting with
two archangels [secret agents], how could she speak to
you? They watch us here. They don't allow us to frat-
ernize with émigrés.

The anecdote raises a question: What if Chekhov had lived
into the Soviet period? Would he have passed the test that
no man or woman should be forced to take? Would he (like
Gorky) have bowed to the dictatorship or would he have re-
sisted and been crushed? One can never predict how anyone
will behave—but everything in Chekhov's life and work expresses an exceptionally strong hatred of force and violence.
In all probability, the libertarian Chekhov would have fared
badly under the Soviets. Almost surely he would not have
died in a posh German hotel room after drinking a glass of
champagne.

Chekhov's death is one of the great set pieces of literary
history. According to an account written by Olga in 1908
(and translated by Benedetti), on the night of July 2, 1904,
Chekhov went to sleep and woke up around one. "He was
in pain, which made it difficult to lie down," Olga wrote,
and continued:

He felt sick with pain, he was "in torment" and for the
first time in his life he asked for a doctor. . . . It was
eerie. But the feeling that something positive had to be

done, and quickly, made me gather all my strength. I woke up Lev Rabenek, a Russian student living in the hotel, and asked him to go for the doctor.

Dr. Schworer came and gently, caringly started to say something, cradling Anton in his arms. Anton sat up unusually straight and said loudly and clearly (although he knew almost no German): *Ich sterbe*. The doctor calmed him, took a syringe, gave him an injection of camphor, and ordered champagne. Anton took a full glass, examined it, smiled at me and said: "It's a long time since I drank champagne." He drained it, lay quietly on his left side, and I just had time to run to him and lean across the bed, and call to him, but he had stopped breathing and was sleeping peacefully as a child."

In another memoir, written in 1922, Olga refined and expanded the death scene thus:

The doctor arrived and ordered champagne. Anton Pavlovich sat up and loudly informed the doctor in German (he spoke very little German), "Ich sterbe."

He then took a glass, turned his face towards me, smiled his amazing smile and said, "It's a long time since I drank champagne," calmly drained his glass, lay down quietly on his left side, and shortly afterwards fell silent forever. The dreadful silence of the night was disturbed only by a large moth which burst into the room like a whirlwind, beat tormentedly against the burning electric lamps, and flew confusedly around the room.

The doctor left, and in the silence and heat of the night the cork suddenly jumped out of the unfinished bottle of champagne with a terrifying bang. It began to grow light, and as nature awoke, the gentle, melodious song of the birds came like the first song of mourning, and the sound of an organ came from a nearby church. There was no human voice, no bustle of human life, only the beauty, calm, and majesty of death.

Awareness of grief, of the loss of such a man as Anton Pavlovich, came only with the first sounds of awakening life, with the arrival of people; and what I experienced and felt, standing on the balcony and looking now at the rising sun, now at nature melodiously awakening, now at the fine, peaceful face of Anton Pavlovich, which seemed to be smiling as if he had just understood something—that, I repeat, still remains for me an unresolved mystery. There had never been such moments as those before in my life, and there never will be again.

Leo Rabeneck set down his own account of the night of July 2, 1904, though he waited fifty-four years to do so. Predictably, it differed in some details from Olga's. In an article called "The Last Minutes of Chekhov," published in Paris in a Russian émigré journal, he recalled that the doctor had asked him to buy oxygen at a pharmacy and had briefly administered it to the dying man. After quoting Chekhov's (or Olga's, as the case may be) "It's a long time since I've drunk champagne," and reporting on the draining of the glass, Rabeneck writes:

> At that moment I heard a strange sound coming from his throat. I saw him lie back on the cushions and thought he did so to breathe more easily. Everything was silent in the room and the lamp grew dimmer. The doctor took Anton Pavlovich's hand and said nothing. After several minutes of silence I thought things were improving and that Anton Pavlovich was out of danger. Then the doctor dropped Anton Pavlovich's hand, and took me to a corner of the room. "It's finished," he said. "Herr Chekhov has died. Will you tell Frau Chekhov?" . . . I went to her. . . . "Olga Leonardovna, the doctor said that Anton Pavlovich has died." She stood like a stone. Then she started to shout in German at the doctor: "It is not true, Doctor, tell me it is not true."

The third eyewitness, Dr. Schwöhrer, left no account, but is quoted in an article dated July 5, 1904, which appeared the following day in the Moscow newspaper *Novostia Dnia*. Its author, an unidentified correspondent (he wrote under the initials S.S.), reported from Badenweiler: "I talked to the doctor who treated A. P. Chekhov here. . . . He was, the doctor said, until the last minute, stoically calm, like a hero. . . . 'When I approached him, he told me peacefully: "Soon, doctor, I am going to die." I wanted to bring him a new supply of oxygen. Chekhov stopped me, saying "There is no need for more. Before they brought the oxygen, I would be dead." ' " Another on-the-scene Russian journalist, Grigori Borisovich Iollos (the Berlin correspondent for the Moscow newspaper *Russkie Vedemosti,* who had become friendly with Chekhov and Olga in Badenweiler and interviewed Olga the day after Chekhov's death), wrote on July 3, 1904: "At one o'clock at night, Anton Pavlovich began to rave, talked of some sailor, then asked something about the Japanese, and after that came back to his senses and with a sad smile told his wife, who was putting an ice-pack on his chest, 'You don't put ice on an empty heart.' " Iollos went on: "His last words were, 'I am dying,' and then, quietly, in German to his doctor, 'Ich sterbe.' His pulse became very weak . . . dying, he sat in bed, bending, supported by pillows; then suddenly he turned on his side and without a sign, without any apparent external sign, his life stopped. An unusually peaceful, almost happy expression appeared on his suddenly youthful-looking face. Through the wide-open window came a fresh breeze, smelling of hay; a light appeared above the forest. No sound anywhere—the small spa town was asleep, the doctor left, a deadly silence filled the house; only the singing of birds could be heard in the room, where, lying on his side, freed from difficulties, a re-markable man and a hard worker, rested on the shoulder of a woman who covered him with tears and kisses."

How Chekhov's biographers have handled the eyewitness testimony (both primary and secondary) in their various renderings of the death scene offers an instructive glimpse into the workings of biographical method.

In *Anton Chekhov: A Life* (1952), David Magarshack writes:

> When the doctor arrived, Chekhov said to him in Ger-man:
>
> "Tod?"
>
> "Oh, no," the doctor replied. "Please calm your-self."
>
> Chekhov was still finding it difficult to breathe and ice was placed on his heart. The doctor sent one of the students for oxygen.
>
> "Don't bother," Chekhov said. "I shall be dead be-fore they bring it."
>
> The doctor then ordered some champagne. Chekhov took the glass, turned to Olga Knipper and said with a smile, "It's a long time since I drank cham-pagne." He had a few sips and fell back on the pillow. Soon he began to ramble. "Has the sailor gone? Which sailor?" He was apparently thinking of the Russo-

Japanese war. That went on for several minutes. His last words were "I'm dying"; then in a very low voice to the doctor in German: "Ich sterbe." His pulse was getting weaker. He sat doubled up on his bed, propped up by pillows. Suddenly, without uttering a sound, he fell sideways. He was dead. His face looked very young, contented and almost happy. The doctor went away.

A fresh breeze blew into the room, bringing with it the smell of newly mown hay. The sun was rising slowly from behind the woods. Outside, the birds began to stir and twitter, and in the room the silence was broken by the loud buzzing of a huge black moth, which was whirling round the electric light, and by the soft sobbing of Olga Knipper as she leaned with her head against Chekhov's body.

Princess Nina Andronikova Toumanova in *Anton Chekhov: The Voice of Twilight Russia* (1937) writes:

Soon Dr. Schwöhrer arrived accompanied by his assistant. They sent for oxygen. Chekhov smiled: It will come too late. A few moments later he became delirious. He spoke about the war and Russian sailors in Japan. This great humanitarian remained true to himself to the end. It was not his family or his friends on whom his last thoughts were centered: it was on Russia and her people. . . . The physicians gave him some champagne. Chekhov smiled again, and then in a distant whisper said: "Ich sterbe." (I am dying.) He sank on his left side. All was ended. Two silent men bent over the motionless form, and, in the stillness of the July night, one could hear only the sobs of a lonely woman.

Daniel Gilles in *Chekhov: Observer Without Illusion* (1967):

Chekhov's fever was so high that he was half delirious: he was raving about some unknown sailor and expressing fear of the Japanese. But when Olga came to put an ice bag on his chest, he abruptly came to himself and gently pushed it away. With a sad smile, he explained: "One doesn't put ice on an empty heart."

Henri Troyat, in *Chekhov* (1984):

Fever had made Chekhov delirious. He went on about a sailor or asked about the Japanese, his eyes shining. But when Olga tried to place an ice bag on his chest, he suddenly regained consciousness and said, "Don't put ice on an empty stomach."

Irene Nemirovsky, in *A Life of Chekhov* (1950):

A huge black moth entered the room. It flew from wall to wall, hurling itself against the lighted lamps, thudded painfully down with scorched wings, then fluttered up again in its blind, impulsive flight. Then it found the open window, and disappeared into the soft, dark night. Chekhov, meanwhile, had ceased speaking and breathing: his life was ended.

V. S. Pritchett, in *Chekhov: A Spirit Set Free* (1988):

They were going to send for oxygen, but Chekhov said he would be dead before it came, so a bottle of champagne was brought. He sipped it and soon began to ramble and he evidently had one of those odd visions that he had evoked in Ward 6. "Has the sailor gone?" he asked. What sailor? Perhaps his sailor in Gusev? Then he said in Russian, "I am dying," then in German, "Ich sterbe," and died at once.

Donald Rayfield, in *Anton Chekhov: A Life* (1997):

He raved of a sailor in danger: his nephew Kolia. Olga sent one of the Russian students to fetch the doctor and ordered ice from the porter. She chopped up a block of ice and placed it on Anton's heart. Dr. Schworer came and sent the two students for oxygen. Anton protested that an empty heart needed no ice and that he would die before the oxygen came. Schworer gave him an injection of camphor.

And, finally, here is Philip Callow, writing in *Chekhov: The Hidden Ground* (1998):

Chekhov was hallucinating, his eyes glittery, talking gibberish about a sailor, about some Japanese. She

tried to put an ice-bag on his chest and he was suddenly lucid, fully conscious. "You don't put ice on an
empty stomach," he told her, like a doctor supervising
a nurse. . . .

Then the doctor, one of those Germans who according to Chekhov followed every rule to the letter, did
something astonishing. He went to the telephone in the
alcove and ordered a bottle of the hotel's best champagne. He was asked how many glasses. "Three," he
shouted, "and hurry, d'you hear?"

In a final effort of courtesy Chekhov sat up, said
"Ich sterbe," and fell back against the pillows. The
champagne arrived, brought to the door by a young
porter who looked as if he'd been sleeping. His fair
hair stood up, his uniform was creased, his jacket half-
buttoned. He entered the room with a silver tray and
three cut-crystal glasses and carried in a silver ice
bucket containing the champagne.

Everything was now in slow motion. The young
man, ignorant of the occasion, could hear someone la-
boring dreadfully for breath in the other room. He
found a place for the tray and glasses and tried dis-
creetly to find somewhere to put the ice-bucket. The
doctor, a big ponderous man with a dense moustache,
gave him a tip and he went through the door as if dazed.

Schwöhrer, not given to displays of emotion, opened
the champagne bottle with his usual quiet efficiency.

And perhaps because he thought it unseemly he eased the cork out so as to minimize the loud pop. He poured three glasses and replaced the cork. Olga freed her fingers for a moment from Chekhov's burning hand. She rearranged his pillow and put the cool glass of champagne against his palm.

As I read these paragraphs, I marveled at the specificity of the new details—the telephone in the alcove, the doctor's "quiet efficiency," the cut-crystal glasses, the sleepy young porter with the half-buttoned jacket. Could Callow have stumbled upon a cache of new primary material in a Moscow attic? I looked for notes at the back of his book and found none. Then something stirred in my memory. I began to feel that I had met the sleepy young porter before. I went to the bookcase and got out a collection of Raymond Carver's stories, *Where I'm Calling From* (1989). In a story entitled "Errand" I read:

Chekhov was hallucinating, talking about sailors, and there were snatches of something about the Japanese. "You don't put ice on an empty stomach," he said when she tried to place an ice pack on his chest. . . .

[Dr. Schwöhrer] went over to an alcove where there was a telephone on the wall. He read the instructions for using the device. . . . He picked up the receiver, held it to his ear, and did as the instructions told him. When someone finally answered, Dr. Schwöhrer ordered a bottle of the hotel's best champagne. "How many glasses?" he was asked. "Three glasses!" the doctor shouted into the mouthpiece. "And hurry, do you hear?" . . .

The champagne was brought to the door by a tired-looking young man whose blond hair was standing up. The trousers of his uniform were wrinkled, the creases gone, and in his haste he'd missed a loop while buttoning his jacket. . . .

The young man entered the room carrying a silver ice bucket with the champagne in it and a silver tray with three cut-crystal glasses. He found a place on the table for the bucket and glasses, all the while craning his neck, trying to see into the other room, where someone panted ferociously for breath. It was a dreadful, harrowing sound. . . .

Methodically, the way he did everything, the doctor went about the business of working the cork out of the bottle. He did it in such a way as to minimize, as much as possible, the festive explosion. He poured three glasses and, out of habit, pushed the cork back into the neck of the bottle. . . . Olga momentarily released her grip on Chekhov's hand—a hand, she said later, that burned her fingers. She arranged another pillow behind his head. Then she put the cool glass of champagne against Chekhov's palm. . . .

"Errand" is one of those hybrid works in which real historical figures and events are combined with invented ones, so that the nonspecialist reader has no way of knowing which is which. In this case, the expert on Chekhov's death that the reader of these pages has become will be able to sort out what Carver invented and what he took from the primary and secondary sources. And he may well conclude that Carver has sinned as greatly against the spirit of fiction as Callow has sinned against the spirit of fact. As Callow does not inform us of what he lifted from Carver, so Carver does not inform us of what he lifted from Olga and the biographers. The young porter is his invention, but Schwöhrer, Rabeneck, Olga, and Anton are not. Nor is he the author of the "plot" of the death scene. The author is Olga. Her powerful narrative is the skeleton on which all the subsequent death scenes hang, Carver's included. Callow's appropriations of Carver's fictionalizations—which are only a degree more imaginative than those of Magarshack, Toumanova, Gilles, et al.—provide a Gogolian twist to the chronicle of the writing of Chekhov's death scene. It is all so dizzyingly mixed up that the moral is a little hard to make out. "Don't put ice on an empty stomach!" may be the one we will have to settle for.

Harvey Pitcher's characterization of Chekhov before his marriage to Olga as "Russia's most elusive literary bachelor" is a given of Chekhov biography. Evidence of Chekhov's many liaisons—from which he always nimbly disengaged himself—was never lacking; the opening of the Soviet archives merely gives this part of his known life a more explicitly sexual shimmer. But one woman involved with Chekhov—Lidia Avilova, a pretty young St. Petersburg wife and mother with literary pretensions—stands out from the rest. Her distinction rests on two facts. One is that she wrote a memoir called *Chekhov in My Life,* chronicling her unhappy love affair with the writer; the other is that the affair was all in her head. *Chekhov in My Life* (published in Russia in 1947 and in America in 1950, in a translation by David Magarshack) is, by all accounts (except David Magarshack's), an exercise in stupendous self-deception, if not a deliberate fraud. Simmons demonstrates in his biography that there was nothing between Avilova and Chekhov beyond bovarysm on her side and embarrassed elusiveness on his. With a thoroughness that sometimes borders on sadism, Simmons tears apart the Avilova memoir, holding up documentary proof of the pathetic untenability of its claim; his savage rout of Avilova runs like a red thread through his otherwise calm biography. (Every time she appears, he can't resist giving her another whack.) Since Simmons, no biographer has been able to be anything but derisive about Avilova's claims. But the memoir alone—it is written in the dialogue-choked style of a girls' romance—gives the show away. "Remember our first meeting?" Chekhov says to her, and incredibly continues, "And do you know—do you know that I was deeply in love with you? Seriously in love with you? Yes, I loved you. It seemed to me that there was not another woman in the world I could love like that. You were beautiful and sweet and there was such freshness in your youth, such dazzling charm. I loved you and I thought only of you." Describing this first meeting—which actually did take place, in 1889, at a dinner party given by Avilova's brother-in-law Sergei Khudekov, the owner and editor of the *Petersburg Gazette* (in which Chekhov had published)—Avilova writes:

Chekhov turned to me and smiled.

"A writer ought to write about what he sees and feels," he said. "Sincerely. Truthfully. I'm often asked what I meant to express by a story. I never answer such questions. My business is to write. And," he added with a smile, "I can write about anything you like. Ask me to write a story about this bottle, and I will write you a story under the title of 'A Bottle.' Living images create thought, but thought does not create images. . . . If I live, think, fight, and suffer, then all this is reflected in whatever I happen to write. . . ."

That Chekhov never spoke these complacent, self-vaunting words will be clear to even the most casual student of Chekhov's life, while the more advanced student will hear in them echoes of things Chekhov actually wrote, or, according to contemporaries, did say. Avilova wrote her memoir around 1940, and she surely could not have remembered what Chekhov said to her fifty years earlier—so she pilfered the published letters and the memoir literature. The comment about "A Bottle," for example, was apparently taken from a passage in Vladimir Korolenko's memoir of Chekhov: " 'Do you know how I write my little stories? Here! . . .' He glanced at the table, took the first object his hand happened to come across—it was an ashtray—put it in front of me, and said: 'Tomorrow, if you like, I'll have a story entitled "The Ashtray." ' "

The letters Chekhov wrote to Avilova herself are even less helpful to her narrative. All but one or two were written in dutiful response to letters of her own (Chekhov made a point of leaving no letter unanswered) and none of them can remotely be said to be love letters. In February 1895, for instance, he wrote Avilova

> . . . I have read both your stories with great attention. "Power" is a delightful story, but I can't help thinking it would be improved if you made your hero simply a landowner, instead of the head of a rural council. As for "Birthday," it is not, I'm afraid, a story at all, but just a thing, and a clumsy thing at that. You have piled

up a whole mountain of details, and this mountain has obscured the sun. You ought to make it either into a long short story, about four folio sheets, or a very short story, beginning with the episode when the old nobleman is carried into the house.

To sum up: you are a talented woman, but you have grown heavy, or to put it vulgarly, you have grown stale and you already belong to the category of stale authors. Your style is precious, like the style of very old writers. . . .

Write a novel. Spend a whole year on it and another six months in abridging it, and then publish it. You don't seem to take enough trouble with your work. . . . Forgive these exhortations of mine. Sometimes one cannot help feeling like being a little pompous and reading a lecture. I have stayed here another day, or rather was forced to stay, but I'm leaving for certain tomorrow.

I wish you all the best.

Yours sincerely,
Chekhov

The Avilova book points up the problem of memoir literature in biography. In this case, the discrepancy between Chekhov's letters and Avilova's clumsy quotations is so huge that one can only dismiss her book as a piece of self-aggrandizing fantasy. A more skillful writer who claimed to have had a secret love affair with Chekhov—or anything else—might not be so easily dismissed. The silence of the famous dead offers an enormous temptation to the self-promoting living. The opportunity to come out of the clammy void of obscurity and gain entrance into posterity's gorgeously lit drawing room through exaggerated claims of intimacy with one of the invited guests is hard to resist. The Korolenko story about the ashtray may itself be an invention, as may many other chestnuts of the Chekhov memoir literature. Memoirs have little epistemological authority. They provide the biographer with the one thing the subject cannot provide and over which the subject usually has little control: the sense of how others see him. The consensus that arises from the memoir literature becomes a part of the subject's atmosphere. But one must be wary of memoirs, factoring in the memoirist's motives, and accepting little in them as fact.

Five

After returning to the hotel from the trip to Gurzuv, I was summoned again to Igor's office. Without looking up from some papers on his desk, he said, "Your suitcase has been found. They will bring it from the airport this evening." It took me a moment to grasp what he had said and to hope it was true. I said thank you and left the office. Something in Igor's manner made me disinclined to question him—and even to feel obscurely in the wrong. Humorlessness as profound as Igor's is unnerving. In fact, the suitcase materialized a few hours later. Someone had rifled it, but had taken nothing. I will never know what happened. Grace, as usual, had arrived on flat, silent feet.

I went to eat dinner at a restaurant Nina had recommended on the hotel's seaside boardwalk. To reach the boardwalk, one descends several hundred feet in an elevator built into the cliff on which the hotel stands. The elevator opens into a long tunnel leading to the beach. The tunnel is dark and dripping, and one's pace quickens the way it does in the sordid transfer tunnels in the New York subway. I met no one in the elevator or the tunnel or along the boardwalk; most of the bars and restaurants and saunas and massage studios were closed. (I later learned from Igor that there were only fifty guests in the hotel; more were expected in the hot, dusty season.) The beach was nearly deserted. I passed a father playing in the dark sand with a shivering child. It was a melancholy scene—not the sweet melancholy of twilight on summer beaches after everyone has gone home but the acrid melancholy of failed enterprises. The sea was gray and still, as if it, too, had lost its will to beguile.

I looked for the restaurant Nina had mentioned—it was called the Krymen—with small expectation of finding it open, but it was open, though without customers. After a search, a tattered handwritten menu in English with strange spellings was produced by an amiable waitress, and soon a delicious dinner of trout and potatoes and cucumber-and-tomato salad was set before me. I am always touched by simple, nicely prepared food, by the idea that a stranger I will never meet has taken care over my dinner, cooking it perfectly and arranging it handsomely on the plate. I feel something friendly and generous wafting toward me. Conversely, I feel the malice and aggression in pretentious, carelessly prepared hotel food; and even the elegant, rigorously prepared dishes served in good restaurants often produce in me a sense of the egotism of their makers: they are doing it for art's sake, not for mine. I have a few times in my life eaten food on the highest level of gastronomy, food imbued with the impersonality of art—from which flowed the same spirit of kindliness and selflessness that I felt at the Krymen.

In "The Wife" (1892), Chekhov describes a meal served at the house of a benign old landowner named Bragin:

> . . . first a cold course of white suckling pig with horse-radish cream, then a rich and very hot cabbage soup with pork in it, with boiled buckwheat . . . pie was served; then, I remember, with long intervals between, during which we drank homemade liquors, they gave us a stew of pigeons, some dish of giblets, roast suckling pig, partridges, cauliflower, curd dumplings, curd cheese and milk, jelly, and finally pancakes and jam.

The narrator, Pavel Andreitch Asorin, is another of Chekhov's flawed heroes who is mysteriously transformed into a decent person. He and his wife, Natalya Gavrilovna, are living together—but not living together—on his country estate. They are like an estranged modern couple who stubbornly continue to occupy a large rent-controlled apartment. The relationship itself has a modern flavor—the raw, close-to-the-bone ambivalence of marriage in the theater of Pinter and Albee. The story centers on a famine in the village, and on the struggle between Natalya, who has organized a successful relief fund, and Asorin, a harsh, abrasive man who attempts to take over her work and run it into the ground because he can't bear the idea of her effectiveness. Asorin's transformation occurs when he awakes from a nap after the gargantuan meal. "I feel as though I had woken up after breaking the fast at Easter," he tells his host, and as he drives home he feels that "I really had gone out of my mind or become a different man. It was as though the man I had been till that day were already a stranger to me." When he arrives home, he goes to his wife and tells her, "I've shaken off my old self with horror, with horror; I despise him and am ashamed of him." He begins a new life of philanthropy and serene relations with Natalya. In the story's final words, "My wife often comes up to me and looks about my rooms uneasily, as though looking for what more she can give to the starving peasants 'to justify her existence,' and I see that, thanks to her, there will soon be nothing of our property left, and we shall be poor; but that does not trouble me, and I smile at her gaily. What will happen in the future I don't know."

Contemporary critics took the line they had taken with "Lights" (and later with "The Duel"), reproving Chekhov for his hero's abrupt, unmotivated change of character. But, after enough time goes by, a great writer's innovations stop looking like mistakes; today we no longer find the transformations of Asorin and Laevsky and Ananyev jarring, and we accept the lacunae in their psychologies as normal attributes of the inhabitants of Chekhov's world. We feel, moreover, that on some level the transformations *have* been prepared for—and it is to this level that a new school of Chekhov criticism has been devoting itself. These critics, who are reading Chekhov's texts "with the attention accorded poetry," as one of them—Julie de Sherbinin, a professor of Slavic literature at Colby College—writes, have come upon an unexpected source of possible meaning in a lode of hitherto uninterpreted material; namely, Chekhov's repeated references to religion. It is a kind of "Purloined Letter" situation: the references to the Bible and to the Russian Orthodox liturgy have always been there, but we haven't seen them, because we took Chekhov at his word as being a rationalist and a nonbeliever. "How could I work under the same roof as Dmitri Merezhkovsky?" Chekhov wrote in July 1903 to Sergei Diaghilev, who had invited him to coedit the journal *The World of Art* with Merezhkovsky. "He is a resolute believer, a proselytizing believer, whereas I squandered away my faith long ago and never fail to be puzzled by an intellectual who is also a believer." And of a Moscow professor named Sergei Rachinsky, who ran a religious elementary school, he wrote (in a March 1892 letter to Shcheglov), "I would never send my children to his school. Why? In my childhood, I received a religious education and the same sort of upbringing—choir singing, reading the epistles and psalms in church, regular attendance at matins, altar boy and bell-ringing duty. And the result? When I think back on my childhood it all seems quite gloomy to me. I have no religion now." However, if we slow the pace of our reading and start attending to every line, we will not fail to pick up the clue in a remark like Asorin's "I feel as though I had woken up after breaking the fast at Easter," or in Ryabovitch's feeling that he has been anointed with oil. Indeed, we will find that whenever a Chekhov character undergoes a remarkable transformation, an allusion to religion appears in its vicinity, in the way mushrooms grow near certain trees in the forest. These allusions are oblique, sometimes almost invisible, and possibly not even conscious.

The Dupin of this new perspective is Robert Louis Jackson, professor of Slavic languages and literatures at Yale, whose writing and teaching on the religious subtext in Chekhov's stories have inspired a generation of younger critics. Chekhov was wary of critics—in "A Dreary Story" he wonderfully satirizes (through his narrator, a professor of medicine) what he calls "serious articles":

> In my childhood and early youth I had for some reason a terror of doorkeepers and attendants at the theater, and that terror has remained with me to this day. . . . It is said that we are only afraid of what we do not un-

derstand. And, indeed, it is very difficult to understand why doorkeepers and theater attendants are so dignified, haughty, and majestically rude. I feel exactly the same terror when I read serious articles. Their extraordinary dignity, their bantering, lordly tone, their familiar manner toward foreign authors, their ability to split straws with dignity—all that is beyond my understanding; it is intimidating and utterly unlike the quiet, gentlemanly tone to which I am accustomed when I read the works of our medical and scientific writers.

Although the tone of the Jacksonian critics could not be quieter or more gentlemanly (or ladylike, as the case may be), Chekhov might well have found their readings intimidating. He would surely marvel at Julie de Sherbinin's reading of "The Teacher of Literature"—a story about a young man's idealization of and subsequent disillusionment with his wife—as a symbolic evocation of the two Marys of Russian Orthodoxy: the virgin mother of God and the harlot Mary of Egypt. And at Alexandar Mihailovic's reading of "Ionich"—a story about the decline of a conscientious, progressive-minded young district doctor with a tendency toward plumpness, into a corpulent monster of avarice and misanthropy—as a fable of self-burial. But he would have to concede that these interpretations are not made of air—the religious allusions from which they take their cue are in the text.

Sherbinin points out in her book *Chekhov and Russian Religious Culture* that "Chekhov was the Russian writer most conversant with the rites and texts of Orthodoxy, as jarring as such a claim might seem, given the centrality of Christian thought to the giants of nineteenth-century letters." It is to the gloomy childhood lived under the rule of the harsh, fanatical father that Chekhov owed this preeminence. While Tolstoy was playing tennis, Chekhov was poring over Scripture or singing *akathistoi*. When he reached adulthood, Chekhov was, perforce, an authority on religion. His writer and artist friends would consult him on fine points of the Bible and the liturgy. The painter I. E. Repin, for example, while working on a painting of Christ in the Garden of Gethsemane, enlisted Chekhov's help in determining whether there had been a moon on the night of the vigil. The mystery of how the grandson of a serf, growing up in semipoverty in an uncouth small town, became one of the world's great writers becomes less mysterious when we take into account the extent to which his religious education prepared him for a literary career. When he began to write his powerful, elliptical stories, he had models ready to hand— the powerful, elliptical stories of the Bible. Chekhov is said to be the father of the modern short story. It might be more accurate (and helpful to contemporary writers wishing to learn from him) to think of him as the genius who was able to cut to the quick of biblical narrative. The brevity, density,

and waywardness of Chekhov's stories are qualities characteristic of Bible stories.

In a story written in 1886 called "Panic Fears," the
unidentified narrator relates three incidents of uncanniness.
The second and third of them turn out to have natural explanations: a railway car with no engine speeding along a
railroad track turns out to be a car that got unyoked from a
train going up a hill, and a big black dog with a sinister,
mythic aura wandering in the forest turns out to be just a
dog who has strayed from its master. But the first mystery—
a strange light glimmering in the window of a church belfry,
which neither comes from within nor is a reflection of anything without—is never solved. The story's position on the
supernatural is unclear. Chekhov could be saying that since
two of the three mysteries had natural explanations, the re-
maining one probably does, too—we just don't know what
it is. Or he could be saying that there are more things in
heaven and earth than rationalism can account for.
Chekhov's allusions to religion are like the strange light.
Since he was secretive about his work, what he "meant" by
his repeated references to the rituals and texts of the religion
he had abjured remains anyone's guess. The Jacksonian critics are careful never to claim that they have found their way
to Chekhov's intentions. They frankly acknowledge the
doubt that is the matrix of their work. But perhaps it is precisely because the whole thing is so mystifying—Does

Chekhov actually believe? Are the religious allusions conscious and purposeful?—that it stimulates such audacious critical thought. Every work of genius is attended by mystery, of course; criticism can no more account for art's radiance than the narrator of "Panic Fears" can account for the sourceless light. But the steady gaze of the Jacksonian critics gives their conjectures a special authority: they do not stray from the text; they keep their eye on the light.

Six

At the beginning of "The Student" (1894), Chekhov offers an arresting aural image: in a swamp "something
alive droned pitifully with a sound like blowing into an
empty bottle." On my first night at the Hotel Yalta, lying in
bed, I heard just such a sound coming in through the window, as relentlessly as a foghorn, but because Chekhov, too,
had heard the call of this night creature, I went to sleep
soothed and happy. The next night, when I heard the sound
again, I realized that no bird or frog could be making a
sound so regular and mechanical. What I was hearing was
obviously coming from a piece of machinery at the swimming pools or one of the outbuildings. My imaginings thus
rearranged, I found the sound irritating and could not fall
asleep for a long time. Incidents from my second day with
Sonia in Moscow—of a piece with the grating persistence of
the sound—came to mind. This was the day of what she
called "city tour"—a drive around Moscow of the sort tour
buses offer, with a canned tour guide's commentary by

Sonia, which she made no effort to disguise. After an hour of what in New York would have been the equivalent of driving past the Empire State Building, the World Trade Center, St. Patrick's Cathedral, and Columbia University, I said I would prefer to receive a perhaps less global, more intimate sense of the city. For instance, could we see Chekhov's grave, and were there any synagogues in Moscow? Sonia sighed and agreed to go to the Novodevichie cemetery, where Chekhov is buried. And, yes, there were two synagogues, though it would be inconvenient to drive to them. At the cemetery, Chekhov's small, modest gravestone had a kind of Slavic Art Nouveau aspect and was in striking contrast to the ornate nineteenth-century monuments and the grandiose Soviet markers, many of them larger-than-life marble busts of the deceased.

In his memoir of Chekhov, Maxim Gorky fretted over the fact that Chekhov's body arrived in Moscow from Baden-weiler in a refrigerated railway car marked "Fresh Oysters." "His enemy was vulgarity," Gorky wrote. "He battled against it all his life. He ridiculed it, depicted it with his sharp, dispassionate pen. . . . And vulgarity took its revenge on him with a vile trick, laying his corpse—the corpse of a poet—in a railway car for 'oysters.' " Other writers have said of the incident that Chekhov would have been amused by it—and also by another fortuitous slight to his corpse: at the Moscow train station, a number of people who had come to escort it to the cemetery followed the wrong coffin, that of a General Keller, which was being accompanied to the cemetery by a military band. But it is doubtful that Chekhov would have been amused. He was not amused at being dead. In a notebook he writes of looking out the window at a corpse being taken to the cemetery, and mentally addressing it thus: "You are dead, you are being carried to the cemetery, and I will go and have my breakfast." The incidents of the car marked "Fresh Oysters" and the following of the wrong coffin were precisely the kind of incidents without consequences that had no interest for Chekhov (in his stories and plays Chekhov sometimes creates an illusion of lifelike pointlessness, but in fact every action has a point)—and are similarly without meaning for students of his life. This ended on the morning of July 3, 1904, and whatever happened thereafter is us having our breakfast.

Sonia's initial negative response to my wish to see a synagogue—like her response to my wish to skip the Armory—presently turned into grudging aquiescence. It turned out that one of the Moscow synagogues was not all that difficult to reach. After Vladimir had parked the car a few yards from the synagogue, a rather gloomy nineteenth-century building, Sonia did not stir and said meaningfully, "I'll stay here." As I approached the synagogue, a group of people came toward me. I took them to be members of the congregation who had come out to greet a visitor. One of the group, whom I assumed to be its leader, came forward from the rest and looked at me eagerly. He was small and unshaven and wore a dark scruffy coat, and when he spoke to me I could not understand what he was saying. After a few moments a word that he repeatedly used became comprehensible. The word was *dollari.* So he and his cohorts were not, after all, characters from a Rabbi Small mystery but beggars. I was surrounded by hands reaching out for the dollar bills I was taking out of my wallet. When my dollars were gone, I gave out ruble bills, and the hands kept reaching out until my wallet was empty. The image came to mind—a horrible one—of someone feeding pigeons. I went into the synagogue, an uninviting place (I have seen such charmless synagogues in America) whose entry hall had announcements posted on its walls, like those posted in college buildings. I met no one; through a distant doorway I glimpsed a room where a stout man in a black suit and white shirt was eating. I started up a staircase, lost heart midway, and came down. Outside on the steps, the beggars were huddled over dark bundles, pulling pieces of cloth from them. They paid no attention to me. Back in the car, I saw Sonia suppress a look of triumph.

My visit to Moscow coincided with the celebration of Victory Day—the fifty-fourth anniversary of the Allied victory over the Nazis. Russia, which lost 27 million people in World War II, was far more absorbed by this occasion than by the current move to impeach President Yeltsin, with which the Western press was intensely involved. In Red Square there was a military parade followed by an evening celebration; thousands of people poured into the square, as if on their way to a rock concert; there were police barricades and a line of portable toilets. I joined the crowd, which was being channeled through a narrow arcade that led to an even narrower street, but when I reached an intersecting street leading away from the square I veered off, giving in to a fear aroused by the thought of the terrible disaster (mentioned in several of the Chekhov biographies) in Khodynka Field in Moscow in the spring of 1896, when nearly two thousand people were crushed to death during a distribution of gifts marking the coronation of Nicholas II.

Earlier in the day, while eating a late lunch in the nearly empty dining room of the Hotel Metropole—a vast hall with an elaborately painted ceiling, marble columns with gilded capitals, ornate chandeliers, potted palm trees, and a central fountain from which a putto and a goose rose—I became aware of a thin old man with a great many medals pinned to his dark jacket, who sat at a table near the fountain. He had finished eating, and was smoking. He was not in uniform; under the jacket was a sweater vest and a shirt and tie. His intelligent face was weary and watchful. He was perhaps the most distinguished-looking man I have ever seen in my life. A bouquet of flowers lay on his table, still in a plastic wrapper, like the bouquets fans bring to the stage at recitals. At a long table near the far wall a group of ten or twelve men and women were reaching the end of a celebratory lunch. From time to time they would rise and give a toast: *"Na zdorov'e! Na zdorov'e!"* Some of the men were in uniform and several wore medals. I wondered why the man with the intelligent face was sitting alone. Had he deliberately separated himself from the others, like Kutuzov separating himself from the deluded military strategists on the eve of the battle of Borodino, or was it an accident that he and they were in the same dining room? On a raised platform a pianist, who looked like Philip Larkin, played American show tunes. The intelligent man sat smoking in a relaxed contemplative attitude. A large tall man appeared at his table and bowed over his hand, almost kissing it; then the two men embraced. At the table of twelve, the toasts had ended and drunken singing had begun. Philip Larkin finished playing and joined the intelligent man at his table.

When I went to pay my bill at the Metropole, there was ahead of me at the cashier a tall, expensively dressed man of around sixty, with a large handsome head, who was in a state. Two young women behind the counter were anxiously looking for his passport. "It's a diplomatic passport with a blue cover," he said exasperatedly. He spoke English with a British accent. "Do you understand? A diplomatic passport. Blue cover." One of the young women continued to shuffle unhappily through a pile of passports (Russian hotels still adhere to the practice most European countries have abandoned: keeping guests' passports for a day or two for inspection by the police), while the other went through a ledger line by line. "They have lost your passport?" I asked. "Yes," he said testily. The young women continued their search. The air was extremely tense. Suddenly, a tall, handsome older woman, wearing a stylish raincoat and a silk scarf with a designer's name on it, appeared at the man's elbow, took in the situation, and said in English, with a slight German accent and a great air of authority, "Go upstairs, Henry, and look in your luggage." Henry obeyed and disappeared into an elevator. The woman—the baroness, as I thought of her—waited for Henry at the side of the counter, while I paid my bill; when my credit card failed to register and I had to produce another, she made a sympathetic comment. The smell of her good perfume wafted toward me. Henry reappeared. Yes, he had found the passport. He was flustered, but he did not apologize to the clerks he had frightened. This was a man of obviously flawed character. What would Chekhov have made of him? Mincemeat, probably. There is a frequently reproduced portrait of Chekhov by an artist named Joseph Braz that is remarkable for its complete failure to capture Chekhov's likeness. (Chekhov said it made him look as if he were sniffing horseradish.) There is an equally inaccurate conception of Chekhov as a writer who condemns no one and "forgives" his characters all their sins. In fact, Chekhov was entirely unforgiving of any of his characters who were cruel or violent—the sadistic Nikita of "Ward No. 6," the infant murderer Aksinya of "In the Ravine," the evil hypocrite Matvey of "Peasant Wives." He was also down on a certain kind of woman he saw as selfish and predatory—Olga in "The Grasshopper," Ariadne in the story of that name, Natasha in *Three Sisters*—and on a certain kind of soulless man: Ionitch in the story of that name, the father in "My Life," the professor in *Uncle Vanya*. (Henry would probably find a place among the foolish and pretentious characters who appear in the early satiric stories and tend to fade from the mature work.) But the flawed characters for whom Chekhov is best known—and who have fostered the idea of his infinite tolerance—are the Laevskys and Gurovs and Ananyevs and Vanyas and Vershinins and Ivanovs, for whom Chekhov sometimes, but not always, arranges a redemptive transformation.

Chekhov's attitude toward these good/bad guys—a singular combination of censoriousness and tenderness—derives, there is reason to think, from Chekhov's relationship to his two older brothers. Two long letters in which Chekhov tells Nikolai and Alexander off, respectively, permit us to move in very close to this relationship.

In the letter to Nikolai (March 1886), Chekhov writes:

> . . . You have often complained to me that people "don't understand you." Goethe and Newton did not complain of that. Only Christ complained of it, but He was speaking of His doctrine and not of Himself. Peo-

ple understand you perfectly well. And if you do not understand yourself, it is not their fault.

I assure you as a brother and as a friend I understand you and feel for you with all my heart. I know your good qualities as I know my five fingers; I value and deeply respect them. . . . You are kind to the point of softness, magnanimous, unselfish, ready to share your last farthing; you have no envy nor hatred; you are simplehearted, you pity men and beasts; you are trustful, without spite or guile, and do not remember evil. You have a gift from above such as other people have not: you have talent. This talent places you above millions of men, for on earth only one out of two million is an artist. Your talent sets you apart: if you were a toad or tarantula, even then, people would respect you, for to talent all things are forgiven.

You have only one failing, and the falseness of your position, and your unhappiness and your catarrh of the bowels are all due to it. That is your utter lack of culture. Forgive me, please, but *veritas magis amicitia.* You see, life has its conditions. In order to feel comfortable among educated people, to be at home and happy with them, one must be cultured to a certain extent. . . .

Cultured people must, in my opinion, satisfy the following conditions:

1. They respect human personality, and therefore they are always kind, gentle, polite, and ready to give in to others. They do not make a row because of a hammer or a lost piece of India-rubber. . . . They forgive noise and cold and dried-up meat and witticisms and the presence of strangers in their homes.

2. They have sympathy not for beggars and cats alone. Their heart aches for what the eye doesn't see. . . .

3. They respect the property of others, and therefore pay their debts.

4. They are sincere, and dread lying like fire. They don't lie even in small things. A lie is insulting to the listener and puts him in a lower position in the eyes of the speaker. They do not pose, they behave in the street as they do at home, they do not show off before their humbler comrades. They are not given to babbling and forcing their uninvited confidences on others. Out of respect for other people's ears they more often keep silent than talk.

5. They do not disparage themselves to rouse compassion. They do not play on the strings of other people's hearts that they may sigh and make much of them. They do not say "I am misunderstood" or "I have become second rate," because all this is striving after cheap effect, is vulgar, stale, false. . . .

6. They have not shallow vanity. They do not care for such false diamonds as knowing celebrities. . . . If they do a pennyworth they do not strut about as though they had done a hundred rubles' worth, and do not brag of having entry where others are not admitted. . . . The truly talented always keep in obscurity among the crowd, as far as possible from advertisement. . . .

7. If they have talent they respect it. They sacrifice to it rest, women, wine, vanity. . . .

8. They develop aesthetic feeling in themselves. They cannot go to sleep in their clothes, see cracks full of bugs on the walls, breathe bad air, walk on a floor that has been spat upon, cook their meals over an oil stove. They seek as far as possible to restrain and ennoble the sexual instinct. What they want in a woman is not a bed-fellow. . . . They want, especially if they are artists, freshness, elegance, humanity, the capacity for motherhood. . . .

And so on. This is what cultured people are like. In order to be cultured and not to stand below the level of your surroundings it is not enough to have read "The Pickwick Papers" and learn a monologue from "Faust."

What is needed is constant work, day and night, constant reading, study, will. . . . You must drop your vanity, you are not a child . . . you will soon be thirty. It is time!

I expect you. . . . We all expect you.

The letter to Alexander (January 2, 1889) is less a set piece, and more disturbingly immediate and intimate (it followed a visit by Chekhov to St. Petersburg, where Alexander lived):

I was seriously angry at you. . . . I was repelled by your *shocking*, completely unprecedented treatment of Natalia Alexandrovna [Natalia Golden, Alexander's second common-law wife] and the cook. Forgive me please, but treating women like that, no matter who they are, is unworthy of a decent, loving human being. What heavenly or earthly power has given you the right to make them your slaves? Constant profanity of the most vile variety, a raised voice, reproaches, sudden whims at breakfast and dinner, eternal complaints about a life of forced and loathsome labor—isn't all that an expression of blatant despotism? No matter how insignificant or guilty a woman may be, no matter how close she is to you, you have no right to sit around without pants in her presence, be drunk in her presence, utter words even factory workers don't use when they see women nearby. . . . A man who is well bred and really loving will not permit himself to be seen without his pants by the maid or yell, "Katka, let me have the pisspot!" at the top of his lungs. . . .

Children are sacred and pure. Even thieves and crocodiles place them among the ranks of the angels. . . . You cannot with impunity use filthy language in their presence, insult your servants, or snarl at Natalia Alexandrovna: "Will you get the hell away from me! I'm not holding you here!" You must not make them the plaything of your moods, tenderly kissing them one minute and frenziedly stamping at them the next. It's better not to love at all than to love with a despotic love. . . . You shouldn't take the names of your children in vain, yet you have the habit of calling every kopeck you give or want to give to someone "money taken from the children." . . . You really have to lack respect for your children or their sanctity to be able to say—when you are well fed, well dressed and tipsy every day—that all your salary goes for the children. Stop it.

Let me ask you to recall that it was despotism and lying that ruined your mother's youth. Despotism and lying so mutilated our childhood that it's sickening and frightening to think about it. Remember the horror and disgust we felt in those times when Father threw a tantrum at dinner over too much salt in the soup and called Mother a fool. There is no way Father can forgive himself all that now. . . .

Natalia Alexandrovna, the cook, and the children are weak and defenseless. They have no rights over you, while you have the right to throw them out the door at any moment and have a good laugh at their weakness if you so desire. Don't let them feel that right of yours.

Anton Chekhov was a younger brother, but he writes here with the calm superiority of a firstborn. He himself has acquired the culture that Nikolai lacks; he does not sit around the house in his underwear and yell for the pisspot. The letters remind us of someone: of von Koren, in "The Duel." They are like notes for the speeches von Koren will make about Laevsky's hopelessness. But the priggish von Koren is not the hero of "The Duel" (as his predecessor, the priggish Dr. Lvov, is not the hero of *Ivanov*). Not being an actual firstborn, Chekhov evidently never felt comfortable in the firstborn's posture of superiority, and expressed his dislike of the censorious side of himself by stacking the deck against his fictional representations of it: von Koren and Lvov are "right," but there is something the matter with them; they are cold fish. Chekhov, in his relationship with his older brothers, brings to mind the biblical Joseph. Chekhov's "sourceless maturity"—like Joseph's—may well have developed during *his* enforced separation from the family. And like Joseph, who wept when he saw his brothers again, in spite of their unspeakable treatment of him, Chekhov's love for his big brothers transcended his anger with them; he evidently never entirely shed his little brother's idealization of them. Out of this family dynamic developed the weak, lovable figure who recurs throughout Chekhov's writing and is one of its signatures. Vladimir Nabokov saw encapsulated in this figure the values lost when Russia became a totalitarian state. In Nabokov's view (put forward in his Wellesley and Cornell lectures in the 1940s and '50s, and collected in *Lectures on Russian Literature*), the Chekhov hero—"a queer and pathetic creature that is little known abroad and cannot exist in the Russia of the Soviets"—"combine[s] the deepest human decency of which man is capable with an almost ridiculous inability to put his ideals and principles into action. . . . Knowing exactly what is good, what is worthwhile living for, but at the same time sinking lower and lower in the mud of a humdrum existence, unhappy in love, hopelessly inefficient in everything—a good man who cannot make good." The émigré Nabokov goes on to write, "Blessed be the country that could produce that particular type of man. . . . [The] mere fact of such men having lived and probably still living somewhere somehow in the ruthless and sordid Russia of today is a promise of better things to come for the world at large— for perhaps the most admirable among the admirable laws of Nature is the survival of the weakest."

Seven

Nina and I are sitting in an outdoor café a few miles down the coast from Oreanda, looking out on another spectacular vista—one on which Gurov and Anna, too, might have gazed—whose focal point is a castle called the Swallow's Nest, built in 1912 (with great difficulty, one would think) atop a rocky cliff dramatically poised over the sea. American popular music, now obligatory in all public places in Russia, fills the air, and puts the Sublime in its place. A waiter brings us Cokes and ham-and-cheese sandwiches. Nina seems to have recovered from her morning's malaise. She eats quickly, and when I offer her the second half of my sandwich—the sandwiches are huge—she accepts it readily. I don't like to think what her normal diet is. She is somewhat overweight, but carries her heaviness well on her large frame. She must have been beautiful in her youth. Her features have a classical regularity, and her cheeks have an appealing flush. Chekhov would have taken note of her. He was acutely sensitive to the appearance of women. In his letters there are constant references—usually negative—to the looks of the women he encountered. Like the women in Badenweiler, the women in Yalta provoked his derision. "I haven't seen one decent-looking woman," he wrote to Olga from Yalta in February 1900. "There are no pretty women," he wrote in September of that year. In December 1902: "I went into town for the first time yesterday . . . all you meet are people who look like rats, not one pretty woman, not one decently dressed." (Fifteen years earlier, writing to his sister about a visit to the Holy Mountains monastery, he paused to say about his fellow pilgrims, "I did not know before that there were so many old women in the world; had I known, I would have shot myself long ago.") Of course, there is irony in Chekhov's presentation of himself as a cold appraiser of female flesh; by the time he lived in Yalta he was clearly out of the running as a rake. But the presence or absence of physical beauty—in male as well as in female characters—rarely goes unremarked in his work. In "The Kiss," Ryabovitch's unprepossessing appearance shapes his identity and determines his fate. In Uncle Vanya, the radiantly good Sonya is similarly burdened; Astrov cannot return her love because he is put off by her plainness. ("You like her, don't you?" Yelena asks him. "Yes, I have respect for her," he replies. "Does she attract you as a woman?" Astrov pauses and then says, "No.") In an essay entitled "Prosaic Chekhov: Metadrama, the Intelligentsia, and Uncle Vanya," Gary Saul Morson, writing of

Chekhov's dislike of histrionics and his regard for prosaic virtue—for "good habits, good manners, and small acts of consideration"—and reading the play as an apotheosis of the prosaic, understands Chekhov to be faulting Astrov for rejecting the estimable, plain Sonya and pursuing the useless, beautiful Yelena. "Chekhov, like Tolstoy, usually regards love based on passion or romance with deep suspicion," Morson writes, and cites the comment of the kindly Dr. Samoilenko in "The Duel": "The chief thing in married life is patience . . . not love but patience." But Morson's compelling essay only demonstrates the difficulty of making any generalization about Chekhov stick. Yes, Chekhov adopts the Tolstoyan position in "The Duel," but in *Uncle Vanya* he swerves sharply from it. In his own life, far from regarding romantic love with suspicion, Chekhov considered it the sine qua non of marriage. He could not have put the matter more plainly than he did in a letter of 1898 to his younger brother Michael (who had been urging him to marry):

> To marry is interesting only for love. To marry a girl simply because she is nice is like buying something one does not want at the bazaar solely because it is of good quality. The most important thing in family life is love, sexual attraction, one flesh; all the rest is dreary and cannot be reckoned upon however cleverly we make our calculations. So the point is not in the girl's being nice but in her being loved.

Indeed, in *Uncle Vanya,* far from faulting Astrov for rejecting Sonya and pursuing Yelena, Chekhov suggests that Astrov can do nothing else. It isn't a matter of choosing between a good course of action and a bad one. In these matters, one has no choice. "Alas, I shall never be a Tolstoyan! In women, what I like above all is beauty," Chekhov wrote to Suvorin in 1891. The words "beauty" and "beautiful" echo throughout the play. Far from celebrating prosaic virtue, *Vanya* mourns its pitiful insufficiency. The action of the play is like the throwing of a stone into a still pond. The "beautiful people"—Yelena and Serebryakov—disturb the life of the stagnant household of Voinitsky and Sonya, stir up the depressed and exhausted Astrov, and then abruptly depart. The waters close over the stone and are still again. *Uncle Vanya* is a kind of absurdist *Midsummer Night's Dream.* Strange events take place, but nothing comes of them. Visions of happiness appear and dissolve. Everything is as it was before. In the heartbreaking speech with which the play ends, Sonya speaks to Vanya of her faith in a "bright, lovely, beautiful" afterlife. Real life remains lusterless, uninteresting, unbeautiful.

In a story written in 1888 called "The Beauties," Chekhov spells out what is coded in *Vanya* and, with characteristic originality, chooses as the vehicle for his meditation on beauty not a professor of aesthetics but a high-school boy. The boy and his grandfather are driving on the steppe on a hot, dusty summer day, and they stop in an

Armenian village to visit a rich and funny-looking Armenian
the grandfather knows. The boy settles himself in a corner
of the Armenian's stifling, fly-filled house, resigned to a
long, boring wait while the grandfather and his host drink
tea. The tea is served by the Armenian's sixteen-year-old
daughter, Mashya, and at the sight of her the boy feels

> all at once as though a wind were blowing over my
> soul and blowing away all the impressions of the day,
> with their dust and dreariness. I saw the bewitching
> features of the most beautiful face I have ever met in
> real life or in my dreams. Before me stood a beauty,
> and I recognized that at the first glance as I should
> have recognized lightning.

The boy notices that he is not the only one dazzled by the
girl's beauty; even his old grandfather is affected. He compares the experience of looking at the girl to that of looking
at a ravishing sunset. He also notices a feeling of

> painful though pleasant sadness. It was a sadness vague
> and undefined as a dream. For some reason I felt sorry
> for myself, for my grandfather and for the Armenian,
> even for the girl herself, and I had a feeling that we all
> four had lost something important and essential to life
> which we should never find again. . . . Whether it was
> envy of her beauty, or that I was regretting that the girl
> was not mine, and never would be, or that I was a
> stranger to her; or whether I vaguely felt that her rare

beauty was accidental, unnecessary, and, like everything on earth, of short duration; or whether, perhaps,
my sadness was that peculiar feeling which is excited in
man by the contemplation of real beauty, God only
knows.

Chekhov's powerful description of aesthetic experience
(the story goes on to a second, less potent illustration of it)
allows us to understand what the stakes were for Astrov and
Voinitsky in their pursuit of the beautiful Yelena (as well as
for Sonya in her pursuit of the handsome Astrov)—and for
Chekhov himself in his apparently trivial attention to
women's looks. "That peculiar feeling"—whether aroused
by a poem or a painting or a piece of music or a view of the
sea or a beautiful girl—was Chekhov's Holy Grail. Although he maintained a pose of ordinariness and was sincere in his valuation of "good habits, good manners, and
small acts of consideration," it was the extraordinary and
the uselessly beautiful that deeply stirred him.

Chekhov's long story "Three Years" (1895) is perhaps
the most profound of his fables of beauty. It is a modern
retelling of the legend of Beauty and the Beast. (It has been
mistakenly taken to be a story about commercial culture in
Moscow.) Laptev, a rich, decent, intelligent, but ugly man,
falls in love with a beautiful young woman named Julia,
who is repelled by him. Chekhov is merciless in his description of Laptev:

[He] knew that he was ugly, and now he felt as though he were conscious of his ugliness all over his body. He was short, thin, with ruddy cheeks, and his hair had grown so thin that his head felt cold. In his expression there was none of that refined simplicity which makes even rough, ugly faces attractive; in the society of women, he was awkward, overtalkative, affected. And now he almost despised himself for it.

Julia turns down Laptev's proposal of marriage, and then decides to master her revulsion and accept him. She feels (as Irina in *Three Sisters* is to feel when she accepts the ill-favored Tuzenbach) that she cannot afford to be choosy. She is moving toward her mid-twenties, she lives at home with a self-absorbed, unloving father, and has no other prospects. Besides, she is kind and feels bad about refusing a decent, honest man. The novella traces the first three years of this sad marriage, narrating it mostly from Laptev's point of view but also, so that we may feel her revulsion, from Julia's. Six months into the marriage, in an exquisitely painful scene in Julia's bedroom, the couple confront their situation.

"I understand your repulsion, your hatred, but you might spare me before other people; you might conceal your feelings."

She got up and sat on the bed with her legs dangling. Her eyes looked big and black in the lamplight.

"I beg your pardon," she said.

He could not utter a single word from excitement and the trembling of his whole body; he stood facing her and was dumb. She trembled, too, and sat with the air of a criminal waiting for explanations. . . .

"You've been my wife for six months, but you haven't a spark of love for me in your heart. There's no hope, not one ray of light! Why did you marry me?" Laptev went on with despair. "Why? What demon thrust you into my arms? What did you hope for, what did you want?"

She looked at him with terror, as though she were afraid he would kill her.

"Did I attract you? Did you like me?" he went on, gasping for breath. "No. Then what? What? Tell me what?" he cried. "Oh the cursed money! The cursed money!"

"I swear to God, no!" she cried, and she crossed herself. She seemed to shrink under the insult, and for the first time he heard her crying. "I swear to God, no!" she repeated. "I didn't think about your money; I didn't want it. I simply thought I should do wrong if I refused you. I was afraid of spoiling your life and mine. And now I am suffering for my mistake. I'm suffering unbearably!"

She sobbed bitterly, and he saw that she was hurt;

and, not knowing what to say, dropped down on the carpet before her.

"That's enough; that's enough," he muttered. "I insulted you because I love you madly." He suddenly kissed her foot and passionately hugged it. "If only a spark of love," he muttered. "Come, lie to me; tell me a lie! Don't say it's a mistake!" . . .

But she went on crying, and he felt that she was only enduring his caresses as an inevitable consequence of her mistake. And the foot he had kissed she drew under her like a bird. He felt sorry for her.

Julia undergoes the terrible suffering of losing the child who has compensated her for her loveless marriage. For many months she can do nothing but grieve. And then, with the inexplicable but inevitable change of heart that occurs in myths and fairy tales, she falls in love with Laptev. However, the Chekhov story does not end like a fairy story. Laptev does not turn into a prince. He remains that peculiar creature—half man, half emblem—by which we mean a Chekhov character. When the magical moment comes, when Julia tells Laptev that she loves him (the scene is in a garden, of course), the prosaic Chekhov appears and coolly breaks the spell: "She had told him she loved him, and he could only feel as though he had been married to her for ten years, and that he was hungry for his lunch."

Eight

Driving back to Yalta from Oreanda, I suggest to Nina, sitting beside me in the rear seat—as I had suggested to Sonia in Moscow—that she buckle her seat belt. Sonia's response had been to inform me icily that only people in front were required to use seat belts. (Vladimir drove without one, buckling up only when he was about to pass a police checkpoint.) I asked Sonia if she thought the rear seat belts were there for decoration. She looked at my strapped-in middle contemptuously. "It is not necessary for you to do that," she said. The ever-agreeable Nina, however, puts on her seat belt, like a good child consenting to try a new food. She translates my von Korenesque lecture on the foolhardiness of driving without a seat belt to the unbelted Yevgeny, who laughs heartily and tells the following anecdote, which he says came from a doctor at a sanitarium where he once worked: "When there is an automobile accident, the person who wasn't wearing a seat belt is found with a leg here, an arm there, the head there. The person who was wearing a seat belt is found in his seat completely intact—and dead."

Illustrations like this of resistance to advances in knowledge appear throughout Chekhov's stories and letters. In a letter to his family written during his journey to Sakhalin (May 1890), he comments on the primitive state of medicine in a village near Tomsk. "Bleeding and cupping are done on a grandiose, brutal scale. I examined a Jew with cancer in the liver. The Jew was exhausted, hardly breathing, but that did not prevent the feldsher from cupping him twelve times." This terrible scene is reprised in the death of Nikolai Tchikildyeev, in "Peasants" (1897). (Chekhov has him cupped twelve times, like the Jew—and then, as if to quantify the difference between life and art, twelve times again.) In the reluctant autobiographical note that Chekhov composed for his medical-school reunion, he spoke of the impact of his medical education on his writing:

It significantly broadened the scope of my observations and enriched me with knowledge whose value for me as a writer only a doctor can appreciate. It also served as guiding influence; my intimacy with medicine probably helped me to avoid many mistakes. My familiarity with the natural sciences and the scientific method has always kept me on my guard; I have tried wherever possible to take scientific data into account, and where it has not been possible I have preferred not writing at all. . . . I am not one of those writers who negate the value of science, and I would not wish to be one of those who believe they can figure out everything for themselves.

Note the many negatives: Chekhov's acknowledgment of the "broadened scope" and "enrichment" the study of medicine has given him is perfunctory, compared to his gratitude for what it has helped him to avoid. As in his letter to Shcheglov about the limits of psychological understanding ("Nothing is clear in this world. Only fools and charlatans know and understand everything"), Chekhov is at pains to dissociate himself from any position of authority. When writing of the horrendous treatment of the Jew with liver cancer, he does not offer an alternative cure. Chekhov spoke of medicine as his wife and writing as his mistress (he later recycled the quip to say that fiction was his wife and the theater his mistress), but he never practiced medicine fulltime, nor attained any particular distinction as a physician. Medicine in Chekhov's day did not have the power to cure that it has only recently begun to wield. Doctors understood diseases they were helpless to cure. An honest doctor would have found his work largely depressing. Simmons speculates that Chekhov's study of medicine originated in an incident of serious illness when he was fifteen—an attack of peritonitis—which led to friendship with the doctor who attended him. Simmons also notes that Chekhov "always attributed to this attack the hemorrhoidal condition which never ceased to trouble him for the remainder of his life." We hear a lot about these hemorrhoids in Chekhov's letters. They evidently bothered him a good deal more than the symptoms of tuberculosis, which appeared as early as 1884, but which he was not to acknowledge as such for thirteen years. "Over the last three days blood has been coming from my throat," he wrote to Leikin in December 1884. "No doubt the cause is some broken blood vessel." And then, two years later, "I am ill. Spitting of blood and weakness. I am not writing anything. . . . I ought to go to the South but I have no money. . . . I am afraid to submit myself to be sounded by my colleagues." It wasn't until March 1897, after a severe hemorrhage at the Hermitage restaurant in Moscow, that he allowed himself to be sounded and diagnosed. Chekhov's knowing–not knowing that he had the disease that killed him was, of course, an expression of denial, but it was also a product of the cruel-kind nature of tuberculosis itself, whose course is not predictable (consumptives have been known to live to old age) and which (as René and Jean Dubos point out in *The White Plague: Tuberculosis, Man and Society*) "waxes and wanes with long periods of apparent remission followed by periods of exacerbation." It was also of a piece with (and may have been implicated in the formation of) Chekhov's stance of insistent uncertainty. If nothing is clear in this world, then everything is possible—even the prospect of health.

The hemorrhage at the Hermitage occurred just as Chekhov and Alexei Suvorin were sitting down to dinner. Blood began pouring from Chekhov's mouth and the flow could not be stemmed. Suvorin took Chekhov to his suite at the Slaviansky Bazaar (where Chekhov was to book Anna Sergeyevna a few years later) and summoned Chekhov's colleague Dr. Nikolai Obolonsky, who could not persuade Chekhov to go to the hospital. The hemorrhage did not abate until morning, when Chekhov insisted on returning to his own hotel, the Moscow Grand (he was now living at Melikhovo and no longer kept a Moscow residence), and on behaving as if nothing had happened. On March 25, after further hemorrhages, he finally entered the clinic of a Dr. Ostroumov, where advanced tuberculosis was diagnosed. The clinic was located near the Novodevichie Cloister, in whose cemetery, seven years later—after writing *Three Sisters, The Cherry Orchard,* "The Lady with the Dog," "The Bishop," "In the Ravine," "Gooseberries," and "Ionitch," among other masterpieces—Chekhov would be buried.

While at the Oustromov clinic, with his characteristic inability to refuse almost any request, Chekhov read the manuscripts of two stories sent him by a stranger, a high-school girl named Rimma Vashchuk, who wanted to know whether she had "a spark of talent." He promptly wrote back to say he liked one of the stories, but that the other, entitled "A Fairy Tale," was "not a fairy tale, but a collection of words like 'gnome,' 'fairy,' 'dew,' 'knights'—all that is paste, at least on our Russian soil, on which neither gnomes or knights ever roamed and where you would hardly find a person who could imagine a fairy dining on dew and sunbeams. Chuck it . . . write only about that which is or that which, in your opinion, ought to be." Stung by Chekhov's criticism, the girl sent him an angry letter, and he, incredibly, wrote to her again from his hospital bed, to patiently explain his criticism. "Instead of being angry, you had better read my letter more carefully," he began. She returned an apology.

During the amended "city tour," on the way to the Novodevichie cemetery, Sonia pointed out a low, long, white building behind some trees as the former Ostroumov clinic, which is now a part of the Moscow University medical school—and, a few blocks later, identified a large red wooden house as Tolstoy's Moscow house. I knew that Tolstoy had visited the debilitated Chekhov two days after his arrival at the clinic, but I hadn't realized how close to the clinic he lived. "We had a most interesting conversation," Chekhov wrote two weeks later to Mikhail Menshikov, of Tolstoy's visit, "interesting mainly because I listened more than I talked. We discussed immortality. He recognizes immortality in its Kantian form, assuming that all of us (men and animals) will live on in some principle (such as reason or love), the essence of which is a mystery. But I can imagine such a principle or force only as a shapeless, gelatinous mass; my I—my individuality, my consciousness—would merge with this mass—and I feel no need for this kind of immortality, I do not understand it, and Lev Nikolayevich was astonished that I don't." Three years later, when Tolstoy was himself ill, and there was a great deal of speculation about the seriousness of his condition, Chekhov wrote again to Menshikov, to say that he had come to think that Tolstoy was not terminally ill, but he added:

His illness frightened me, and kept me on tenterhooks. I am afraid of Tolstoy's death. If he were to die, there would be a big empty place in my life. To begin with, because I have never loved any man as much as him. I am not a believing man, but of all beliefs I consider his the nearest and most akin to me. Second, while Tolstoy is in literature it is easy and pleasant to be a literary man; even recognizing that one has done nothing and never will do anything is not so dreadful, since Tolstoy will do enough for all. His work is the justification of the enthusiasms and expectations built upon literature. Third, Tolstoy takes a firm stand, he has an immense authority, and so long as he is alive, bad taste in literature, vulgarity of every kind, insolent and lachrymose, all the bristling, exasperated vanities will be in the far background, in the shade. Nothing but his moral authority is capable of maintaining a certain elevation in the moods and tendencies of literature, so-called . . .

Chekhov had met Tolstoy only a few times, but "when he spoke about Tolstoy," Gorky writes in his memoir of Chekhov, he "always had a particular, barely detectable, affectionate and bashful smile in his eyes. He would lower his voice as if talking of something spectral, mysterious, something requiring mild and cautious words." As for Tolstoy, "he loved Chekhov," Gorky wrote, "and always when he looked at him his eyes, tender at that moment, seemed to caress Chekhov's face." However, Tolstoy did not love Chekhov's plays. He is reported to have said to Chekhov, "You know, I cannot abide Shakespeare, but your plays are even worse."

Chekhov, in turn, had a few reservations about Tolstoy's writings. He didn't like the characterization of Napoleon in *War and Peace* ("As soon as Napoleon is taken up, we get a forcing of effect and a distortion to show that he was more stupid than he actually was," he wrote to Suvorin in 1891), and took issue with certain of Tolstoy's pronouncements in *The Kreutzer Sonata*. "Tolstoy treats that which he does not know and which he refuses to understand out of sheer stubbornness," he wrote Alexei Pescheyev in 1890. "Thus his statements about syphilis, about asylums for children, about women's aversion to copulation, etc., are not only open to dispute, but they actually betray an ignorant man who, in the course of his long life, has not taken the trouble to read two or three pamphlets written by specialists." But he felt constrained to add: "And yet all these defects scatter like feathers before the wind; one simply does not take account of them in view of the merits of the novel. . . ." Chekhov had also gone through a period of belief in Tolstoy's ideas about nonviolence and then had become skeptical of them. But, as is evident from his comments about the threat of Tolstoy's death, he never lost his sense of Tolstoy's artistic preeminence.

Earlier in the day, in the Arbat, once an elegant shopping district and now, much reduced in size, an undervisited tourist trap of souvenir shops, secondhand stores, and kitsch art galleries, Sonia had stopped before a small oil painting of a vase of lilacs.

"This is good," she said.

"Are you going to buy it?" I asked.

Sonia shook her head. With a modest little smile, she explained that she painted herself and therefore recognized good art when she saw it. She had paused simply to register her appreciation. She painted on weekends and during vacations, specializing in still lifes and portraits.

My journalist's portrait of Sonia as a latter-day Natasha Prozorov was taking shape. Her remarks about art contributed a nice Natashaesque touch. Of course, not everything Sonia said and did had this kind of value. In fact, most of what she said and did went unrecorded in my notebook. Journalistic subjects are almost invariably stunned when they read about themselves in print, not because of what is revealed but because of what has been left out. Journalists, like the novelists and short-story writers who are their covert models, practice a ruthless economy. The novice who wishes to be "fair" to his subjects and to render them in all their unruly complexity and contradictoriness is soon disabused. The reality of characters in fiction—and of their cousins in journalism—derives precisely from the bold, almost childlike strokes with which they are drawn. Tolstoy renders Anna Karenina through her light, resolute step, her eagerness, her friendliness and gaiety, her simple, elegant dress. He confines her thoughts and actions to a range of possibility that no person in life is confined by. Chekhov's realism, as we have seen, is of a different order; his economy is even more stringent, his strokes even blunter. His Natasha is a figure about whom we know almost nothing in particular—she is simply a concentration of coarseness and bullying willfulness. In the first act, before she shows her true colors, appearing to be only a girl from the town who feels awkward in the house of her aristocratic fiancé, she undergoes a small mortification. Olga, the oldest sister, points out to her that her green sash doesn't go with her pink dress, that "it looks queer." Natasha's taste in dress has already been deplored by Masha, in something of the way Chekhov deplored the dress of German women. But, on another level, something more serious than bad taste is at issue in Olga's reprimand, namely, bad faith, as denoted by the color green and its association with the Serpent. (According to Chekhov's stage directions, Olga addresses Natasha about the sash "with alarm," suggesting that she has "recognized" Natasha.) In the story "In the Ravine," written a year earlier, and also about the takeover of a household by a ruthless daughter-in-law, Chekhov actually describes the woman in question as a snake.

> Aksinya had naive gray eyes that rarely blinked and a naive smile played continually on her face. And in those unblinking eyes, and in that little head on the long neck, and in her slenderness there was something snakelike; all in green but for the yellow on her bosom, she looked with a smile on her face as a viper looks out of the young rye in the spring at the passersby, stretching itself and lifting its head.

Aksinya is perhaps the most evil character in Chekhov. In a scene that matches, and, in its shocking unexpectedness, possibly surpasses the horror of the blinding of Gloucester,

Aksinya scalds to death a baby who stands in the way of her ascendancy. Natasha comes nowhere near this level of evilness. She is unbearable, but she would never commit murder. Aksinya is all in green, Natasha wears only a green sash—a touch of evil. My Sonia—clearly a Natasha rather than an Aksinya—might fittingly have worn a green scarf. However, I am bound to report that she wore a red scarf (over a white angora sweater). Nonfiction may avail itself of the techniques of elision and condensation by which fiction achieves its coherence, but is largely barred from the store of mythopoetic allusion from which fiction derives its potency. Even Chekhov, when writing nonfiction, doesn't write like Chekhov. The book he wrote reporting on a three-month visit to the prison colony of Sakhalin in the summer of 1890, for example, is a worthy and often interesting work, but rarely a moving one, and never a brilliant one.

The Island of Sakhalin isn't an artistic failure, since Chekhov had no artistic ambitions for it. He saw it as a work of social and natural science, and he even considered submitting it to the University of Moscow medical school as a dissertation attesting to his qualifications to teach there. (The idea was broached to the dean of the medical faculty by Grigory Rossolimo, and scornfully turned down.) It ran serially in the journal *Russian Thought* in 1893, and was published as a book in 1895. There are occasional Chekhovian passages, but not many; it is a book largely of information. In 1897, when he was in Nice for his health, Chekhov was asked by an editor to write a story "on a subject taken from life abroad"; he declined, explaining, "I am able to write only from memory, I never write directly from observed life. I must let the subject filter through my memory, until only what is important and typical in it remains in the filter." In the book on Sakhalin, Chekhov wrote from file cards and scholarly books and reports. His customary artist's fearlessness gave way to a kind of humility, almost a servility, before the ideal of objectivity and the protocols of scientific methodology. Like a convict chained to a wheelbarrow (one of the punishments at Sakhalin), he drags along the burden of his demographic, geographic, agricultural, ethnographic, zoological, and botanical facts. He cannot omit anything; his narrative line is constantly being derailed by his data. In his autobiography for Rossolimo, Chekhov registered his awareness that "the principles of creative art do not always admit of full accord with scientific data; death by poison cannot be represented on stage as it actually happens." In the Sakhalin book, the conflict between science and art is almost always resolved in science's favor. Chekhov tells it like it is, and allows his narrative to go where his mountain of information pushes it, which is all over the place, and ultimately nowhere. Chekhov's horror at the harshness and squalor of life in the colony, his contempt for the stupidity and callousness of the administration, and his pity for the convicts and settlers sometimes does break through the posture of scientific detachment. But in rendering the sufferings on this island of the damned, Chekhov could not achieve in three hundred pages what he achieved in a four-page passage at the end of his story "The Murder" (1895) about Sakhalin convicts in fetters loading coal onto a steamer on a stormy night.

If the trip to Sakhalin yielded no work of literary distinction, its personal (and eventual literary) significance for Chekhov was momentous. He needed to go on a journey. In a letter to Suvorin written on May 4, 1889, from a rented dacha in the Ukraine, he wrote, "There is a sort of stagnation in my soul. I explain it by the stagnation in my personal life. I am not disappointed, I am not tired, I am not depressed, but simply everything has suddenly become less interesting. I must do something to rouse myself." It is impossible to know, of course, what Chekhov meant by the stagnation in his personal life, but it seems likely that his malaise was connected to the final illness (from tuberculosis) of his brother Nikolai, whom he had been nursing since March, first in Moscow and then at the dacha. The letter of May 4 characteristically makes no mention of the rigors of the death watch, but three glancing references to Nikolai tell the story of Chekhov's sense of stuckness: "I'm in a good mood, and if it weren't for the coughing painter and the mosquitoes—even Elpes formula is no protection against them—I'd be a perfect Potyomkin," and, later, "Bring me some banned books and newspapers from abroad. If it weren't for the painter, I'd go with you," and, a few lines down, "Lensky [an actor in the Maly Theater] has invited me to accompany him on tour to Tiflis. I'd go if it weren't for the painter, who's not doing any too brilliantly." Nikolai died on June 17, and in September Chekhov completed his powerful and long "A Dreary Story," about an eminent professor who comes to the end of his life and finds it frighteningly meaningless; he realizes that he lacks a ruling idea with which to make sense of his existence. The atmosphere of the work is like a taste of tin in the mouth, the fatigue behind the eyes produced by something unbearable. That it was written by a man in mourning is not surprising; perhaps *only* a man in mourning could have written a tale of such sour painfulness. Simmons speculates that Nikolai's death from tuberculosis forced Chekhov to confront the probability of his own death from the disease and, further, that "A Dreary Story" reflects Chekhov's own need for a ruling idea. On October 4, 1888, in a much-quoted letter, Chekhov had written of his independence of any such need:

> I am not a liberal, not a conservative, not a believer in gradual progress, not a monk, not an indifferentist. I should like to be a free artist and nothing more, and I regret that God has not given me the power to be one.

> I hate lying and violence in all their forms. . . . I regard
> trademarks and labels as a superstition. My holy of
> holies is the human body, health, intelligence, talent,
> inspiration, love, and the most absolute freedom—
> freedom from violence and lying, whatever forms they
> may take. This is the program I would follow if I were
> a great artist.

A year later, Chekhov was no longer so comfortable with
his artist's freedom. At the end of 1889, he abruptly
dropped literature and began to make preparations for the
six-thousand-mile journey to Sakhalin, at the easternmost
end of the continent. In letters to his baffled friends,
Chekhov gives various high-minded reasons for making the
trip—to fulfill his debt to science, to rouse the conscience of
an indifferent public—but the explanation that has the
greatest ring of truth is the one he gave to Shcheglov in a letter of March 22: "I am not going for the sake of impressions
or observations, but simply for the sake of living for six
months differently from how I have lived hitherto."

The letters Chekhov wrote during the two-and-a-half-
month journey are some of the best he has left us. They permit us to see, as if in a movie with a large budget for special
effects, the hardships he endured as he made his way across
the continent, first by train and riverboat, and then (for the
largest part of the trip—nearly three thousand miles) by frail

open horse-drawn vehicles on rutted and sometimes washed-out roads. (The Trans-Siberian Railroad did not yet exist.) He traveled, day and night, in frigidly cold weather and endless spells of rain. He suffered from hunger and cold and painful shoes. Before he became accustomed to it, the jogging and lurching of the open carriage made his bones ache. For a consumptive to undertake such a trip would seem like a form of suicide. But, strangely, Chekhov didn't sicken; on the contrary, he thrived. As the journey progressed, he stopped coughing and spitting blood, and started feeling really well (even his hemorrhoids subsided). In *The White Plague,* the Duboses devote a chapter to some of the odder forms of therapy that were thought up during the premodern period of tuberculosis. One of these was the horseback-riding cure, popular in the eighteenth century. They cite several cases of patients (one of them John Locke's nephew) who recovered from tuberculosis after strenuous daily riding, and note a Dutch physician's recommendation that consumptives "of the lower classes who were confined to sedentary occupations endeavor to find employment as coachmen." They go on to write of a cobbler who did become a coachman. "He was well as long as he remained in the saddle (on the box) but lost his health when he returned to cobbling." Chekhov remained well until he returned to Moscow, in the fall of 1890, when his poor health promptly returned. ("It's a strange business," he wrote to Suvorin on

December 24. "While I was traveling to Sakhalin and back I felt perfectly well, but now, at home, the devil knows what is happening to me. My head is continually aching, I have a feeling of languor all over, I am quickly exhausted, apathetic, and worst of all, my heart is not beating regularly.")

In his letters during the trip, he exulted over his endurance. On June 5, during a stopover in the Siberian town of Irkutsk, where he slept in a real bed and had a bath ("The soapsuds off my head were not white but of an ashen brown color, as though I were washing a horse"), he wrote to Leikin:

> From Tomsk to Krasnoyarsk was a desperate struggle through impassable mud. My goodness, it frightens me to think of it! How often I had to mend my chaise, to walk, to swear, to get out of my chaise and get into it again, and so on! It sometimes happened that I was from six to ten hours getting from one station to another, and every time the chaise had to be mended it took from ten to fifteen hours. . . . Add to all that hunger, dust in one's nose, one's eyes glued together with sleep, the continual dread that something would get broken in the chaise. . . . Nevertheless I am well content, and I thank God that He has given me the strength and opportunity to make this journey. I have seen and experienced a great deal, and it has all been very new and interesting to me not as a literary man,

but as a human being. The Yenissey, the Taiga, the stations, the drivers, the wild scenery, the wild life, the physical agonies caused by the discomforts of the journey, the enjoyment I got from rest—all taken together is so delightful that I can't describe it. . . .

On June 20, Chekhov exulted again to Leikin from a ship on the Amur River:

I have driven with horses more than four thousand versts. My journey was entirely successful. I was in good health all the time and lost nothing of my luggage but a penknife. I can wish no one a better journey. The journey is absolutely free from danger, and all the tales of escaped convicts, of night attacks, and so on are nothing but legends, traditions of the remote past. A revolver is an entirely superfluous article. Now I am sitting in a first-class cabin, and feel as though I were in Europe. I feel in the mood one is in after passing an examination.

Chekhov arrived at Sakhalin on July 11, and remained there for three months, traveling all over the island and using the device of a census to gain entrance into prisons and settlers' huts. (Simmons theorizes that the project of a scientific investigation of the colony was itself an after-the-fact rationale to justify his journey to his friends—and to himself.) Chekhov set about his work with characteristic energy and zeal. He managed to interview thousands of people; along with the convicts and settlers, he interviewed the indigenous Gilyaks and Ainus. By October, he was more than ready to leave.

Back in Moscow in December (he made the return journey by ship from Vladivostok—through Hong Kong, Ceylon, India, Egypt, and Turkey—to Odessa) he wrote to Suvorin, "I know a great deal now, but I have brought away a horrid feeling. While I was staying in Sakhalin, I had only a bitter feeling in my inside as though from rancid butter; and now, as I remember it, Sakhalin seems to me a perfect hell. For two months I worked intensely, putting my back into it; in the third month, I began to feel ill from the bitterness I have spoken of, from boredom, and the thought that the cholera would come from Vladivostok to Sakhalin, and that I was in danger of having to winter in the convict settlement." But a week later he wrote to Suvorin, "How wrong you were when you advised me not to go to Sakhalin . . . what a sour creature I would be now if I had sat at home. Before my journey *The Kreutzer Sonata* seemed to me to be an event, but now it seems to me absurd and ridiculous. Either I've grown up because of my journey or I have gone crazy—the devil knows which."

On the eve of Chekhov's heroic journey a complication had arisen that almost ruined it. An artist named N—, "a nice but tedious man," wanted to travel with him. Chekhov enlisted Suvorin's aid, writing, "To refuse him my company I haven't the courage, but to travel with him would be simple misery." Chekhov went on, "Be my benefactor, tell N— that I am a drunkard, a swindler, a nihilist, a rowdy character, and that it is out of the question to travel with me, and that a journey in my company will do nothing but upset him." "When one is traveling one must be absolutely alone," Chekhov wrote to his sister on June 13, concluding his complaints about a trio of traveling companions—an army doctor and two lieutenants—he had picked up somewhere along the way and now wished to shed. He had begun to complain about the trio in a previous letter to Masha (June 7): "I like silence better than anything on the journey, and my companions talk and sing without stopping, and they talk of nothing but women." Chekhov finally shed the officers by traveling first-class on the Amur River steamer, where they had booked second-class.

That he had picked them up in the first place is consistent with his lifelong inconsistency in regard to solitude. (On the boat, he actually sought out the officers and had tea with them.) He liked silence, but he also didn't like it. He complained about trying to write in a room where someone was banging on the piano, a baby was crying, and someone else was asking his advice about a medical matter; but when the house was silent he would ask his brother to play the piano. He complained about the number of guests at Melikhovo, but also said he couldn't live without guests. ("When I'm alone, for some reason I become terrified, just as though I were alone in a frail little boat on a great ocean," he wrote to Suvorin in June 1889.) At the end of his life, when he felt stuck in Yalta, as he had felt stuck with the dying Nikolai, he complained about the crowd of visitors he had—and about his feeling of isolation. He was a restless man—perhaps because he understood too well what rest represented. "Life is only given us once, and one wants to live it boldly, with full consciousness and beauty," the consumptive narrator of "An Anonymous Story" (1893) says. Chekhov lived only forty-four years, and during the last third of his life he was surely conscious of the likelihood of a premature death. Those of us who do not live under such a distinctly stated sentence of death cannot know what it is like. Chekhov's masterpieces are always obliquely telling us.

Nine

Chekhov's decision to write a book of nonfiction about his journey to Sakhalin, instead of allowing the trip to develop into fiction in his interior darkroom, may have been influenced by the fact that he had already written a masterpiece of fiction about a journey. This was the long story "The Steppe" (1888), the first Chekhov story to appear in a literary journal (as opposed to a newspaper) and the work that catapulted him into the ranks of major Russian writers. The story chronicles a summer journey across the steppe of a nine-year-old boy named Yegorushka, accompanying his merchant uncle, Ivan Ivanitch Kuzmitchov, and an old priest, Father Christopher Sirevsky, who are taking a convoy of wagons filled with wool to a distant town, where the wool will be sold and the boy put in school. Along the way, they search for a mysterious, powerful entrepreneur of the steppe named Varlamov, on whom the sale of the wool obscurely depends. "I describe the plain, its lilac vistas, the sheep breeders, the Jews, the priests, the nocturnal storms, the inns, the wagon trains, the steppe birds and so on," Chekhov wrote to Grigorovich on January 12, 1888, while composing the story. But he was nervous about it:

> . . . I'm ending up with something rather odd and much too original. Since I'm not used to writing anything long and am constantly, as is my wont, afraid of writing too much, I've gone to the other extreme. All the pages come out compact, as if they had been condensed, and impressions keep crowding each other, piling up, and pushing one another out of the way. The short scenes . . . are squeezed tightly together; they move in an unbroken chain and are therefore fatiguing; instead of a scene I end up with a dry, detailed list of impressions, very much like an outline; instead of an artistically integrated depiction of the steppe, I offer the reader an encyclopedia of the steppe.

Chekhov sounds as if he could not quite come to terms with his own originality. He is like a resistant reader of an avant-garde work. The compression about which he frets is, of course, the compression that is the signature of his mature work. The writing that is "very much like an outline" is precisely the writing that demands "the attention accorded poetry." It is prose as pared down—and as charged—as poetry.

Early in "The Steppe" (subtitled "The Story of a Jour-

ney") Chekhov draws a crucial contrast—one that will
hover over the story—between the merchant and the priest
as travelers. Kuzmitchov is like the businessmen one sees
today on planes and trains working on laptops and talking
on cell phones. He is oblivious of his surroundings. He only
wants to get there. "Fanatically devoted to his work,
Kuzmitchov always, even in his sleep and at church when
they were singing 'Like the cherubim,' thought about his
business and could never forget it for a moment; and
now"—the men are taking a nap—"he was probably
dreaming about bales of wool, wagons, prices, Varlamov."
Father Christopher, in contrast,

> had never in all his life been conscious of anything
> which could, like a boa constrictor, coil about his soul
> and hold it tight. In all the numerous enterprises he
> had undertaken in his day, what attracted him was not
> so much the business itself, but the bustle and the con-
> tact with other people involved in every undertaking.
> Thus in the present expedition, he was not so much in-
> terested in wool, in Varlamov, or in prices, as in the
> long journey, the conversations on the way, the sleep-
> ing under a chaise, and the meals at odd times. . . . He
> must have been dreaming of . . . all sorts of things that
> Kuzmitchov could not possibly dream of.

How should one live? Like a Kuzmitchov or a Father
Christopher? The story is borne like a canopy on these two

poles of possibility. Kuzmitchov is desperate to find Varlamov, who has always just left the place at which the travelers have arrived. He searches for him the way we search in
dreams for someone we will never find. Father Christopher
is calm: "A man isn't a needle—we shall find him." As
Kuzmitchov looks at him "almost with hatred," the priest
faces east and for a quarter of an hour Kuzmitchov must
wait while he recites his psalms for the day. The quest for
Varlamov threads its way through the pages of "The Steppe"
with a similar lack of urgency, as though Chekhov were reluctant to allow a conventional plot device to coil about his
narrative. But when Varlamov finally comes into view—a
short, gray older man on a small horse, showing his dis-
pleasure to a subordinate who has not followed orders—he
is a figure of electrifying authority. "It's people like that the
earth rests upon," a peasant says of him. Varlamov's face has

> the same expression of businesslike coldness as Ivan
> Ivanitch's face, the same look of fanatical zeal for busi-
> ness. But yet what a difference could be felt between
> him and Kuzmitchov! Uncle Ivan Ivanitch always had
> on his face, together with his businesslike reserve, a
> look of anxiety and apprehension that he would not
> find Varlamov, that he would be late, that he would
> miss a good price; nothing of that sort, so characteris-
> tic of small and dependent persons, could be seen in
> the face or figure of Varlamov. This man made the
> price himself, was not looking for anyone, and did not

depend on anyone; however ordinary his exterior, yet in everything, even in the manner of holding his whip, there was a sense of power and habitual authority over the steppe.

You will have noted the word "Uncle." It is Yegorushka who has been observing Varlamov and whose thoughts Chekhov records. The consciousness of the boy—who is not yet either a Kuzmitchov or a Father Christopher, but possesses both the former's hysterical anxiety and the latter's capacity for pleasure—is the lens through which most of the events of "The Steppe" are seen. (Chekhov reserves portions of the text for an omniscient narrator.) It might seem that Chekhov has exceeded the bounds of plausibility in endowing a nine-year-old child with such astuteness and such complexity of thought. But, on rereading the passage, we see that Chekhov has made no misstep. While a nine-year-old could not write the passage or speak it in those words, he could think it. Chekhov intercepts his thought—as he intercepted that of Ryabovitch in "The Kiss"—but does no violence to it as he turns it into prose. His acute sensitivity to the difference between unexpressed and expressed thought guides him in his risky feat. Two of Yegorushka's other interior monologues reveal more about Chekhov's poetics. The first takes place at the beginning of the story, as the chaise bearing the boy and the merchant and the priest drives out of their village past a cemetery where, amid the white crosses and tombstones, cherry trees grow.

> Yegorushka remembered that when the cherries were in blossom those white patches melted with the flowers into a sea of white; and that when the cherries were ripe the white tombstones and crosses were dotted with splashes of red like bloodstains. Under the cherry trees in the cemetery Yegorushka's father and granny, Zinaida Danilovna, lay sleeping day and night. When Granny had died she had been put in a long narrow coffin and two pennies had been put upon her eyes, which would not keep shut. Up to the time of her death, she had been brisk, and used to bring soft rolls covered with poppy seeds from the market. Now she did nothing but sleep and sleep. . . .

Here—perhaps because he has only just introduced Yegorushka—Chekhov points up the naïveté of his interior monologuist. Later he will not feel the need to remind us so insistently that we are in the mind of a child. But again he performs the tour de force of endowing the boy with thought exceeding his expressive capacities, while never going outside the repertoire of what a child can imagine and feel.

The second example is one of the strangest passages in literature. Chekhov may well have been thinking of it when he worried that "The Steppe" was "much too original." The journey takes place during a time of extreme heat and drought. The travelers have stopped to eat and rest, and while the men are napping, the hot and bored boy tries to amuse himself. Suddenly, in the distance, he hears a woman singing a song that is "subdued, dreary and melancholy, like a dirge and hardly audible."

> Yegorushka looked about him, and could not make out where the strange song came from. Then, as he listened, he began to fancy that the grass was singing; in its song, withered and half dead, it was without words, but plaintively and passionately, urging that it was not to blame, that the sun was burning it for no fault of its own; it urged that it ardently longed to live, that it was young and might have been beautiful but for the heat and the drought; it was guiltless, but yet it prayed forgiveness and protested that it was in anguish, sad and sorry for itself.

There is a kind of anthropomorphism-within-anthropomorphism here. As the writer attributes words to the boy that the boy would not utter, the boy attributes thoughts to the grass that the grass could not "think." In rendering the boy's excruciating empathy with the grass, it is almost as if Chekhov were mimicking his own act of sympathetic imagination. Echoes of another "much too original" text—the Book of Isaiah, with its images of landscapes cruelly withered by God to teach his stiff-necked people not to cross him and its analogizing of the life of man to the life of grass— may be heard in the passage. We do not know whether Chekhov was intentionally (or even unconsciously) evoking Isaiah, but when the Kuzmitchov party meets a barefoot old shepherd with a loincloth and a crook—"a regular figure from the Old Testament"—or stops at an inn owned by an obsequious Jew named Moisey (Moses), or encounters water coming out of rock, we can hardly avoid the thought that the journey is some kind of latter-day Exodus. The storm that is the real climax of the work seems like one of the more showy magical stunts of the Old Testament deity. It begins with a casual display of power—"someone seemed to strike a match in the sky; a pale phosphorescent streak gleamed and went out"—and mounts to awe-inspiring extremes of violence. The boy, atop one of the wool wagons, is exposed to the storm's fearful wind, rain, lightning, and thunder, and becomes ill with chills and fever; he recovers after the priest rubs (anoints) him with oil and vinegar.

The boy is a rather characterless character, a kind of generic child, expressing the passivity and sadness of childhood, and recording impressions in something of the way a camera does. (The melancholy of photography has been noted by several of its practitioners.) When he is at the inn of the obsequious Moisey, he notes its gloominess and ugliness and the "disgusting smell of kerosene and sour apples" that permeates it. Like the boy at the stifling house of the

Armenian in "The Beauties" (which Chekhov wrote later in the year), Yegorushka has an unexpected brush with beauty at the horrible inn. He is lying half asleep on a sofa when a beautiful young noblewoman, dressed in black and sending forth "a glorious scent," appears and kisses him on the cheeks. She is the Polish Countess Dranitsky, a rich local landowner, about whose semiannual balls (at which tea is made in silver samovars, and strawberries and raspberries are served in winter) the boy had already heard at home, and about whom he will now entertain pleasurable fantasies. She, too, is looking for Varlamov (neither the boy nor we ever learn why). When the boy first sees her, the image of a graceful poplar he had seen standing alone on the steppe comes into his mind "for some reason." The reason is clear enough. The Countess, too, stands alone in the story—its only aristocrat and emblem of the culture and gentility that the boy's mother is sending him away from home to acquire. The boy has also heard about the extraordinary table clock in the Countess's drawing room: a golden rider on a rearing golden horse with diamond eyes brandishes his sword to right and left as the clock strikes. When we meet Varlamov he rides a small nonrearing horse and brandishes a whip. He is the self-made New Man whom we will meet again in Chekhov's writings, most memorably as Lopakhin in *The Cherry Orchard*. Neither is unsympathetic; Chekhov had no illusions about the days of rearing golden horses and riders with slashing swords. Another typical character is Dymov, one of the drivers of the wool wagons, an obnoxious young bully, under whose provocation Yegorushka's passivity gives way to fury and loathing. Dymov is a relatively mild version of the helplessly violent man we will meet again in later works—Solyny in *Three Sisters,* and Matvey Savich in "Peasant Wives," for the two worst examples—and for whom Chekhov retained a child's pure hatred. A character who has no successors—who is a kind of flash of unrepeatable inspiration—is a driver named Vassia, who has been horrifyingly mutilated by his earlier work in a match factory—his jaw is being eaten away—but who has a remarkable and wonderful power:

> His sight was extraordinarily keen. He was so long-sighted that the brown steppe was for him always full of life and interest. He had only to look into the distance to see a fox, a hare, a bustard, or some other animal keeping a distance from men. There was nothing strange in seeing a hare running away or a flying bustard—everyone crossing the steppes could see them; but it was not vouchsafed to everyone to see wild animals in their own haunts when they were not running nor hiding, nor looking about them in alarm. Yet Vassia saw foxes playing, hares washing themselves with their paws, bustards preening their wings and hammering out their hollow nests. Thanks to this keenness of sight, Vassia had, besides the world seen by everyone, another world of his own, accessible to no one

else, and probably a very beautiful one, for when he saw something and was in raptures over it it was impossible not to envy him.

"There are many places that will be understood by neither critics nor the public; they will seem trifling to both, not meriting attention, but I anticipate with pleasure the two or three literary epicureans who will understand and value these same places, and that is enough for me," Chekhov wrote to Y. P. Polonsky in January 1888, in another of the defensive letters he felt impelled to write to friends while working on the most ambitious project he had yet undertaken. In an essay entitled "Chekhov's 'Steppe': A Metapoetic Journey" (1987), a literary epicurean named Michael Finke fulfills Chekhov's expectations of being understood with an almost Vassia-like perspicacity. He sees what no previous critic has seen—motifs and allusions tucked into "places" of no apparent significance (such as the floor of a shop marked with kabbalistic symbols or two peculiar pictures on the wall of the reception room in Moisey's inn)— and his essay permanently changes our view of the story as an inspired but inchoate effort, written before Chekhov was in full possession of his artistic powers. Conventional criticism of "The Steppe" has taken Chekhov's self-criticism at face value (almost always a mistake), and missed the figure in the carpet that Finke's reading reveals. The story, as it appears under Finke's high-powered lens, proves to be a work of breathtaking artistic unity. Details that seemed random and incoherent fall into place as elements of an intricate design—but one so cleverly hidden it is small wonder that no one saw it for a hundred years. "If a story is to seem at all original," Finke writes, "its order must somehow be disguised, known only in retrospect, and those laws of necessity governing the function of detail must be masked." "The Steppe," as Finke suggests, is "a sort of dictionary of Chekhov's poetics," a kind of sample case of the concealed literary weapons Chekhov would deploy in his work to come.

In the short story "The Schoolmistress," written ten years later, we see how the compression that made Chekhov so uneasy in 1888 was now his modus operandi. It is another emblematic story of a journey, but this one is the mere return day trip of a spinster schoolteacher, Marya Vassilyevna, from the town where she goes to get her monthly salary. The teacher is one of the pathetic drudges who (as Chekhov learned at Melikhovo) taught in Russia's district schools in the nineteenth century (and may still do so in the twenty-first). The life of a schoolteacher

is a hardworking, an uninteresting, life, and only silent, patient cart horses like Marya Vassilyevna could put up with it for long; the lively, nervous, impressionable people who talked about a vocation and serving the idea were soon weary of it and gave up the work.

The teacher is traveling in a horse-drawn cart, driven by an old coachman named Semyon. It is April, with traces of winter, "dark, long, and spiteful," still on the ground, but with delicious signs of spring in the air—to which, however, Marya Vassilyevna is impervious. She has taken this trip monthly for thirteen years and "whether it were spring as now, or a rainy autumn evening, or winter, it was all the same to her." Like Kuzmitchov obsessively thinking about wool and prices and Varlamov, Marya obsessively thinks about the examinations she must prepare her students for, about the brutality of the school watchman, about the indifference of Zemstvo officials, about the difficulty of obtaining firewood for the schoolroom. Chekhov pauses to tell us that Marya Vassilyevna was orphaned at ten, and can remember almost nothing of her early life, in a large flat in Moscow, near the Red Gate. Then he gives us an unforgettable image: Marya's one relic from her childhood is a photograph of her mother, but it has faded so badly that nothing remains visible but the hair and the eyebrows. We feel we have seen such photographs, but have never before thought of them as metaphors for fading memory.

As the teacher and the coachman travel through an increasingly mired terrain, they meet a landowner named Hanov, driving a carriage with four horses. Marya Vassilyevna is acquainted with Hanov, and so are we: he is our old friend the good man who cannot make good, cousin to

Ivanov, Laevsky, Astrov, Vershinin. In this version, he is "a man of forty with a listless expression and a face that showed signs of wear, who was beginning to look old, but was still handsome and admired by women. He lived in his big homestead alone, and was not in the service; and people used to say of him that he did nothing at home but walk up and down the room whistling, or play chess with his old footman. People said, too, that he drank heavily."

After greeting Hanov, the schoolteacher goes back to her obsessions. But the thought floats into her mind that Hanov is attractive. When the road grows so muddy that Semyon and Hanov have to get down and lead their horses, she watches Hanov and thinks, "In his walk there was something, just perceptible, that betrayed in him a being already touched by decay, weak, and on the road to ruin." She gets a whiff of alcohol, and goes on to feel "dread and pity for this man going to ruin for no visible cause or reason, and it came into her mind that if she had been his wife or sister she would have devoted her whole life to saving him from ruin." She pursues the fantasy—and quickly dismisses it.

The mere thought that he and she might be close to one another and equals seemed impossible and absurd. In reality, life was arranged and human relations were complicated so utterly beyond all understanding, that when one thought about it one felt uncanny, and one's heart sank. "And it is beyond all understanding," she thought, "why God gives beauty, this graciousness, and sad, sweet eyes to weak, unlucky, useless people—why they are so charming."

Hanov turns off and Marya's obsessions again take over her thoughts. Her bare life, Chekhov notes, "was making her grow old and coarse, making her ugly, angular, and awkward, as though she were made of lead. . . . No one thought her attractive, and life was passing drearily, without affection, without friendly sympathy, without interesting acquaintances." The journey itself is as vexing as the life:

> Semyon kept picking out the driest and shortest way, first by a meadow, then by the backs of the village huts; but in one place the peasants would not let them pass, in another, it was the priest's land and they could not cross it, in another, Ivan Ivonov had bought a plot from the landowner and had dug a ditch around it. They kept having to turn back.

Eventually, they stop at a rough tavern; outside, wagons filled with large bottles of crude sulfuric acid stand on ground covered with snow and dung. The peasants drinking within show small respect for the schoolteacher. She is practically one of them. On the last leg of the journey the travelers have to cross a river. Semyon chooses to go through the water rather than over a bridge a few miles away. When

they enter the river, the horse goes in up to his belly, and
Marya's skirt and sleeve get soaked, and so do the sugar and
flour she bought in town. On the other side, at a railway
crossing, they find the barrier down. The schoolmistress gets
out of the cart and stands shivering on the ground. The end
of the story is less than a page away. Chekhov writes:

> [The village] was in sight now, and the school with its
> green roof, and the church with its crosses flashing in
> the evening sun; and the station windows flashed too,
> and a pink smoke rose from the engine . . . and it
> seemed to her that everything was trembling with cold.
>
> Here was the train; the windows reflected the
> gleaming light like the crosses on the church: it made
> her eyes ache to look at them. On the little platform
> between two first-class carriages a lady was standing,
> and Marya Vassilyevna glanced at her as she passed.
> Her mother! What a resemblance! Her mother had had
> just such luxuriant hair, just such a brow and bend of
> the head. And with amazing distinctness, for the first
> time in those thirteen years, there rose before her mind
> a vivid picture of her mother, her father, her brother,
> their flat in Moscow, the aquarium with little fish,
> everything to the tiniest detail; she heard the sound of
> the piano, her father's voice; she felt as she had been
> then, young, good-looking, well-dressed, in a bright
> warm room among her own people. A feeling of joy

and happiness suddenly came over her, she pressed her hands to her temples in an ecstasy, and called softly, beseechingly:

"Mother!"

At this moment Hanov and his carriage arrive at the crossing, "and seeing him she imagined happiness such as she had never had, and smiled and nodded to him as an equal and a friend, and it seemed to her that her happiness, her triumph, was flowing in the sky and on all sides, in the windows and on the trees. Her father and mother had never died, she had never been a schoolmistress, it had been a long, tedious, strange dream and now she had awakened . . ."

The vision abruptly vanishes, like the sun going down in winter. Marya gets back into the cart and proceeds to the village and to her dismal life. The long, tedious, strange dream goes on.

The previous year, Chekhov had written *Uncle Vanya*. (Or probably had; he was extremely secretive about its composition, perhaps because of its relationship to *The Wood Demon,* a bizarrely poor play he wrote in 1889 and wished to disown but from which *Uncle Vanya* unquestionably derives.) The schoolmistress's brief fantasy about marriage to the handsome, depressed, alcoholic Hanov is a kind of shorthand version of Sonya's deep, hopeless love for the handsome, depressed, alcoholic Astrov. At the end of the play, after the professor and Elena and Astrov have gone and Sonya and Vanya are left to live out their lives as silent, patient cart horses, Sonya, too, has an ecstatic vision. She has abandoned hope of earthly happiness, but imagines an afterlife "that is bright, lovely, beautiful. We shall rejoice and look back at these troubles of ours with tenderness, with a smile—and we shall rest. I have faith, Uncle; I have fervent, passionate faith." We do not know whether Marya Vassilyevna has faith, but the church, with its crosses flashing in the setting sunlight, is the fulcrum of her ecstasy. (Chekhov used this image in several other stories, including "Three Years" and "Lights.") A Finkean or perhaps a Jacksonian reading of "The Schoolmistress" would also take note of Marya's baptism in the river and of the fish in the Moscow apartment. As always, Chekhov's allusions to religion are inconclusive. They mark important moments, but they are written in pencil. As always, and unlike Tolstoy, Chekhov leaves the question of what it all means unanswered. He raises it, but then—as if remembering that he is a man of science and a rationalist—seems to shrug and walk out of the room.

Ten

The second day of my stay in cold, idle St. Petersburg had been scheduled to begin with a visit to one of Catherine the Great's palaces, but when I told Nelly that palaces didn't especially interest me, she—unlike Sonia when I balked at the Armory—simply asked what I wanted to do instead. As with Nina, I felt an immediate rapport with Nelly. She was younger than Nina—she had a fresh, round face, and short, wavy brown hair, and looked to be in her fifties. She was not poor, and was more sophisticated, and more reserved. When I asked her about herself, she told me just so much and no more: that she was a widow (her husband had died of cancer two years earlier); that she had recently remodeled her apartment; that she had a tomcat; that she had been a university teacher of languages, and then had gone into the travel business, originally working for Intourist and now for a private agency called Esperance; that she bought her clothes abroad. She performed her job as guide and translator with beautiful precision, as if it were a piano sonata; throughout my stay in the city, she seemed to know exactly when to explain and when to be silent; when to be present and when to vanish.

She and the driver, Sergei, met me at the St. Petersburg airport, a place that time seems to have forgotten. The terminal, of an early totalitarian-modern style, is worn and faded, leached of all menace. It was empty and silent. Here and there along the stone-floored corridor leading to passport control, a spindly potted palm inclined toward a dusty window. No other flight had come in—perhaps ours was the flight of the day or week—and it took no time to get through the formalities. Sergei picked up my suitcase, and he and Nelly led me to the car, which was parked in a small lot directly in front of the terminal. Was I in Mother Russia or at the Brewster, New York, train station?

Driving in from the airport, we passed ugly, flimsy housing projects, which grew less ugly and more substantial as we neared the city. Nelly said that the apartments in the outlying projects, built post-Khrushchev, were incredibly tiny. The projects closer to the city, which had been built in the Stalin period, had decent-size apartments and were much coveted. My hotel, the Astoria, built in the late nineteenth century and recently renovated, was as empty as the airport. Normally, American tourists fill the city's hotels and restaurants, but fear that anti-American feeling had been aroused by our recent mindless bombing of the Chinese embassy in Belgrade had kept them away. (I, in fact, encountered no anti-American feeling during my stay in Russia.) My handsome room was furnished with imperial-style antiques and looked out on the dull-gold dome of St. Isaac's cathedral, which was designed by an Italian architect and has a beautiful Florentine austerity. During the Soviet period, the cathedral housed a Museum of Atheism, but now it had resumed Russian Orthodox services, as churches throughout the former Soviet Union were doing. Nelly told me that under Communism belief was tolerated among those willing to remain in society's lowliest positions; but to rise in the hierarchy it was necessary to be an atheist. Atheism was the "official religion," she said. On the way to the hotel, she had pointed out a church in which the Soviets had dug a swimming pool—now being filled in.

The next morning, when Nelly asked me to propose a substitute for the visit to Catherine's palace, I had one ready, and a few minutes later Sergei pulled up in front of a small house on a narrow side street where Dostoevsky had once lived, and which was now the Dostoevsky Museum. We bought tickets and walked through a series of small rooms filled with conventional Victorian furniture and objects. If one stretched one's imagination, one could read into the slight dreariness and somberness of the rooms some connection to the author of *Crime and Punishment* and *The Brothers Karamazov*. But they could just as well have been occupied by a government clerk or a retired army officer.

Chekhov never met Dostoevsky, who died in 1881, at the age of sixty, and was not drawn to his writing; as he exalted Tolstoy, he edged away from Dostoevsky. In March 1889, he wrote to Suvorin, "I bought Dostoevsky at your store, and am now reading him. Pretty good but too long-winded and too indelicate. There is much that is pretentious." And one day in 1902, while out fishing on an estate in the Urals, Chekhov said to a friend, "We're such a bone-lazy people. We've even infected nature with our laziness. Look at this stream—it's too lazy to move. See how it twists and turns, all because of laziness. All our famous 'psychology,' all that Dostoevsky stuff, is part of it, too. We're too lazy to work, so we invent things." (The friend was Alexander Tikhonov, a twenty-two-year-old student of mining engineering, who later became the Soviet writer Alexander Serebrev. His book *Time and People,* in which the passage appears, has not been translated into English. I quote from an extract in David Magarshack's biography.) Satiric references to "that Dostoevsky stuff" recur in Chekhov's stories. In his not all that funny sendup of detective fiction "The Swedish Match" (unlike any other story by Chekhov, it seems too long), an eager young sleuth, trying to pin a murder on the victim's elderly sister, tells the examining magistrate, "Ah, you don't know these old maids, these Old Believers! You should read Dostoevsky!" Or in "Neighbors" (1892), a pathetic loser named Vlassich is trapped in a "strange marriage in the style of Dostoevsky"—to a prostitute, naturally. But Chekhov's relationship to Dostoevsky is not quite as simple as it may appear. Literary influence is a complicated business, and does not hinge on like or dislike. It is not always conscious. There is reason to think that Chekhov, though he disliked Dostoevsky, drew on him nevertheless. "Neighbors" is one of the works in which this influence—unconscious or merely covert, who can say?—may be glimpsed.

The story is narrated by a young man named Pyotr Mihailich, whose sister, Zina, has been seduced by the pathetic Vlassich. Vlassich is separated but not divorced from the Dostoevskian tart, and Zina has defiantly moved in with him on his run-down farm. Pyotr rides out to the farm intending to horsewhip his sister's seducer—and stays to eat strawberries with the errant pair. He finds he cannot hate Vlassich. Indeed, he "was fond of Vlassich; he was conscious of a sort of power in him." At the end of the story, as Pyotr Mihailich rides home, he berates himself. "I am an old woman! I went to solve the question and I have only made it more complicated—there it is!" Making it more complicated is, of course, Chekhov's own stock in trade; but when, near the end of "Neighbors," the story takes a joltingly strange turn, we may wonder whether he realized just how complicated he was making it. (We do know that Chekhov himself was critical of the story; he wrote to Suvorin that he thought it shouldn't have been published.)

The strange turn comes when Zina, making nervous, black-humorous conversation with her brother, says of her new home, "It's a charming house. . . . There's some pleasant memory in every room. In my room, only fancy, Grigory's grandfather shot himself. . . . And in this dining-room, somebody was flogged to death." Vlassich then tells the gruesome story of a sadistic Frenchman called Olivier, who had leased the house and had "sat here at this table drinking claret" while stable boys beat to death a young divinity student Olivier disliked. Pyotr Mihailich, angry at himself for his inaction, thinks, "Olivier behaved inhumanly, but one way or another he did settle the question, while I have settled nothing and have only made it worse. . . . He said and did what he thought right, while I say and do what I don't think right; and I don't know really what I do think. . . ." Chekhov knew very well what he thought of violence—he hated it—and Pyotr Mihailich's perverse approval of Olivier's violence seems more in "the style of Dostoevsky" than in that of Chekhov. A Raskolnikov or a Stavrogin might have rationalized such brutality, but surely not soft, nebbish Pyotr Mihailich. The lapse may help us untangle the knot of Chekhov's relationship to Dostoevsky. That Chekhov was concerned with the question of evil that reverberates through Dostoevsky's novels is clear from works like "Ward No. 6," "In the Ravine," and "Peasant Wives." He may have found Dostoevsky pretentious, but he might not have been impelled to write these stories had not

The Brothers Karamazov and *Crime and Punishment* come into his ken. As Chekhov divided his life between the time he was beaten and the time he was no longer beaten, so his stories break down into those that take place in the universe where "everything is permitted" and those set in the world of ordinary human beings who cannot stop making each other miserable but do not step over the line into barbarism. He had begun to look into the abyss early in his writing career; among the contributions to the humor magazines there are grim little tales that point directly to the mature works of despair. One of these is the seven-page story "Because of Little Apples" (1880), in which another sadist watches another beating. This time, a landowner catches a young engaged peasant couple eating apples in his orchard, and devises the amusing punishment of forcing first the girl to beat the boy and then the boy to beat the girl. When it's the boy's turn, his sadistic impulses are set off, and in his "ecstasy" he cannot stop beating the girl. Chekhov will reuse this Dostoevskian psychological insight in "Peasant Wives." Here the evil hypocrite Matvey watches the husband of the woman he has seduced go out of control and beat and kick the woman he loves until she collapses. The beating in "Because of Little Apples" stops (when the landowner's daughter appears on the scene) before the girl is seriously injured but not before the relationship between the pair is irreparably damaged. The boy and the girl walk out of the orchard in opposite directions and never see each other again. The scent of Dostoevsky that subtly emanates from the story was picked up by Robert Louis Jackson. In an essay called "Dostoevsky in Chekhov's Garden of Eden" Jackson plausibly connects the story's "motifs of physical cruelty and spiritual disfiguration, the absolute humiliation of the individual, and sadistic delight in cruelty" to Dostoevsky's work in general, and, in particular, to a chilling story about the destruction of innocence called "A Christmas Party and a Wedding." He believes that the nineteen-year-old author of "Little Apples" was already thoroughly conversant with Dostoevsky's work (which would mean that he was rereading it when he made his comment to Suvorin) and that the parallels between "A Christmas Party" and "Little Apples" are too obvious to ignore.

Chekhov never again wrote so directly about the catastrophe that occurred in the biblical first garden. His gardens thenceforth are prelapsarian, sites of redemption and renewal, freedom and air. References to the Serpent's gift of sexual guilt are relegated to out-of-the-way corners of the narrative, and lodged in brief, unemphatic references to the eating of fruit. Zinaida, the sexy heroine of "An Anonymous Story," who diverts the hero from a revolutionary mission, is introduced lying on a sofa eating a pear, for example; the temptress antiheroine of "Ariadne" eats apples and oranges in the middle of the night (as well as roast beef, ham, and men); and, in the most famous example, Gurov eats watermelon—a display not only of his callousness but an allusion to the transgressive sex that has just taken place. The lovers in "An Anonymous Story" and "Ariadne" end up as alienated as the peasant couple in "Little Apples." It is worth recalling about Anna and Gurov that after they have sex it is touch and go whether they, too, will go off in opposite directions. When Anna assumes her Mary Magdalene attitude, and reproaches herself for being "a vulgar, contemptible woman," Gurov feels "bored, already, listening to her" and "irritated by the naive tone, by this remorse, so unexpected and inopportune." But, as roués know how to do, he controls his irritation, and sweet-talks Anna out of her uninteresting remorse. Most significant, he gets her out of the room. It is the trip to Oreanda—to the sea, mountains, open sky—that marks the beginning of the peaceful love that is to arise between them, and of his transformation. Dostoevsky's heavy shadow doesn't fall on this story, of course—the most delicate and fragrant of Chekhov's tales—or on the largest part of his work. And, where it does fall, it is so oblique that we need the help of a literary radiologist like Jackson to make it out.

When we left the Dostoevsky Museum, Nelly directed Sergei to drive us to the nearby Anna Akhmatova Museum, located in a wing—the former servants' wing—of an eighteenth-century palace called the Fountain House, where the poet lived on and off for thirty years. The museum is filled with representations (photographs, paintings, drawings, sculptures) of a strikingly beautiful and elegant woman—tall, slender, with dark bangs, always unsmiling—who achieved fame as an avant-garde poet in her early twenties and lived to become one of the heroines of the tragedy of Russian Communism. Though a child of privilege, Akhmatova, born in 1889 (as Anna Andreyevna Gorenko—in 1911 she took the pen name Akhmatova, after a Tatar princess who was her great-grandmother), chose not to join the aristocrats, artists, and writers who left Russia after the revolution, and threw in her lot with those who remained to see the tragedy through. Her fortitude in the face of suffering and loss—her first husband was shot by the Bolsheviks, her only son was imprisoned three times, for a total of thirteen years, her friend and fellow poet Osip Mandelstam died in a labor camp, as did her third husband—and the major poetry she quietly produced during three decades as a banned (and thus destitute) writer have given her legendary status. Isaiah Berlin, recalling an extraordinary night-long conversation he had with Akhmatova in the autumn of 1945, when she was fifty-six, wrote: "She did not in public, nor indeed to me in private, utter a single word against the Soviet regime: but her entire life was what Herzen once described virtually all Russian literature as being—one uninterrupted indictment of Russian reality."

Akhmatova's poem "Requiem," perhaps the best known

of her works in the West, was written during one of her son's incarcerations, at the height of the Stalin terror, and takes us into this reality with chilling directness:

> You should have been shown, you mocker,
> Minion of all your friends,
> Gay little sinner of Tsarskoye Selo,
> What would happen in your life—
> How three-hundreth in line, with a parcel,
> You would stand by the Kresty prison,
> Your fiery tears
> Burning through the New Year's ice.
> Over there the prison poplar bends,
> And there's no sound—and over there how many
> Innocent lives are ending now.

Akhmatova herself escaped arrest, though not the fear of it by which life in Russia was defined during the Stalin years. In a memoir of Akhmatova, Nadyezda Mandelstam, the widow of the poet, writes: "Of everything that happened to us, what was most significant and powerful was the fear and what it produced—a loathsome feeling of disgrace and impotence. There is no need to try to remember this; 'this' is with us always." Mandelstamova goes on to record Akhmatova's stoicism and courage and consistent good conduct during a period when just being decent was to take your life in your hands.

Berlin writes of Akhmatova as "immensely dignified, with unhurried gestures, a noble head, beautiful, somewhat severe features, and an expression of immense sadness . . . she moved and looked like a tragic queen." One is somehow not surprised to learn that this Niobe "worshiped Dostoevsky," and did not care for Chekhov:

> She asked me what I read: before I could answer she denounced Chekhov for his mud-coloured world, his dreary plays, the absence in his world of heroism and martyrdom, of depth and darkness and sublimity—this was the passionate diatribe, which I later reported to Pasternak, in which she said that in Chekhov "no swords flashed."

But when Berlin revisited the Soviet Union in 1956, and spoke with Akhmatova on the telephone (she did not dare see him, for fear of endangering her son, who was briefly out of prison), she told him that she had reread Chekhov, and acknowledged, he writes, that "at least in 'Ward 6' he had described her situation accurately, hers, and that of many others." This, too, is not surprising. It only underscores the divide between Chekhov's Dostoevskian examinations of extreme situations—works full of "depth and darkness and sublimity," "heroism and martyrdom"—and those situated on the blessedly "dreary" other side of the barbed wire.

At the museum, a gray-haired woman with a crocheted

shawl and a wool cap attached herself to Nelly and me—
one of the army of retired women with insufficient pensions
who are glad to find ill- or unpaid work in museums—and
recited an earnest and naïve spiel about the poet's life. The
largest part of the museum is given over to Akhmatova's
early life: to the paintings, drawings, sculptures, and photographs (among them a drawing by Modigliani, whom
Akhmatova met in Paris in 1911) that Akhmatova's contemporaries, ravished by her interesting beauty, tripped over
each other to make; and to exhibits of books and manuscripts from the period when she was still able to publish. In
addition, there are rooms that supposedly reconstruct the
various periods when Akhmatova lived at the Fountain
House—first with her second husband, Vladimir Shileilko,
an Assyriologist; then with her third husband, the art histo-
rian Nikolai Punin (and with his ex-wife and child; such was
communal apartment life in those days); then (after her separation from Punin) in a room of her own in the Punin
apartment. When her friend Lydia Chukovska visited her in
this room in 1938, she found that its "general appearance
. . . was one of neglect, chaos. By the stove an armchair,
missing a leg, ragged, springs protruding. The floor
unswept. The beautiful things—the carved chair, the mirror
in its smooth bronze frame, the lubok prints on the walls—
did not adorn the room; on the contrary, they only empha-
sized its squalor further." By the end of the war, when

another friend, Natalia Roskina, visited the room, the beautiful things were gone. "The circumstances in which Akhmatova was then living could not be described as impoverished, for poverty implies having a little of something. She had nothing," Roskina writes in a memoir of 1966. "There was a small, old desk in her room and an iron bed covered with a shabby blanket. The bed was obviously hard and it was obvious that the blanket provided no warmth."

Akhmatova's room in the museum has none of the squalor of Chukovska's description or the bleakness of Roskina's. It is of a piece with the elegant young beauty in the drawings and paintings and sculptures and photographs. It is sparsely furnished, but as if by willful design rather than out of pathetic necessity. Only choice and rare pieces of furniture and objects have been admitted: a leather-covered chaise with curved wooden legs on which a small black leather suitcase mysteriously rests; a glass-fronted rosewood cabinet with a few interesting pieces in it (a fan, a strange bottle with a crystal stopper, a porcelain statuette of Akhmatova in her youth); a chair with a white fringed shawl thrown over it; a carved chest with a couple of leather-bound books and three *commedia dell'arte* rag dolls lying on it. The room looks out on the palace's grassy, tree-filled courtyard. There is no trace in it of the line that stood in front of the Kresty prison or of the corpulent old woman Akhmatova became in the last years of her life. Shrines operate under a kind of reverse Gresham's law: beauty, youth, order, pleasure drive out ugliness, old age, disorder, suffering. In Paris, in 1965, Akhmatova was shown an article in an émigré journal that spoke of her as a martyr, and she protested, "If they want to write about me over here, let them write about me the way they write about other poets: this line is better than that one, this is an original use of imagery, this image does not work at all. Let them forget about my sufferings." Chekhov sounded a similar note of asperity in the summer of 1901 in a letter to Olga: "You write, 'my heart begins to ache when I think of the silent, deep well of melancholy within you.' What nonsense is this, my darling? I am not melancholy and never have been and feel tolerably well and when you're with me I feel absolutely fine." Akhmatova was fourteen when Chekhov died. Had he lived he undoubtedly would have met her in St. Petersburg literary society, and would not have complained about her looks or her clothes. He might or might not have liked her poetry, but he would have known better than anyone what she meant when she said, "Let them forget about my sufferings."

Eleven

I left the Mariinsky Theater in St. Petersburg after the second act of an exceptionally trite and listless *Carmen,* but not before mingling with the intermission crowd in one of the buffets, where children in velvet party clothes and adults in evening dress crowded around refreshment stands and carried away glasses of champagne and fruit drinks and dishes of ice cream and small plates piled with sandwiches and pastries and chocolates wrapped in cornucopias of colored foil. I felt a stir of memory, a flutter of the romance theater held for me when I was myself a child in a velvet dress.

The role of theater in relieving the bleak joylessness of Chekhov's childhood has been noted by his biographers. He and his classmates would go to the Taganrog Theater to see plays or hear operettas, sitting in the cheap seats, and sometimes even wearing dark glasses and their fathers' coats to avoid expulsion. (Unaccompanied schoolboys were not allowed in the theater. A boyhood memory doubtless inspired the moment in "The Lady with the Dog" when two schoolboys, illicitly smoking on the stair landing of a provincial theater, look down and see Gurov emotionally kissing Anna's face and hands.)

Chekhov began writing plays at an early age. (The untitled manuscript of the half-baked play we call *Platonov* surfaced in the 1920s and was thought to have been written when he was twenty or twenty-one.) In the English-speaking world, Chekhov is better known as a dramatist than as a story writer. Everyone has seen a *Cherry Orchard* or an *Uncle Vanya*, while few have even heard of "The Wife" or "In the Ravine." But Chekhov was never comfortable as a playwright. "Ah, why have I written plays and not stories!" he wrote to Suvorin in 1896. "Subjects have been wasted, wasted to no purpose, scandalously and unproductively." A year earlier, when the first draft of *The Seagull* had been coolly received by theater people and literary friends, Chekhov had written to Suvorin, "I am not destined to be a playwright. I have no luck at it. But I'm not sad over it, for I can still go on writing stories. In that sphere I feel at home; but when I write a play, I feel uneasy, as though someone were peering over my shoulder."

Chekhov wrote "The Steppe" (1888) in a month and "The Name-Day Party" (1888) in three weeks; it took him almost a year each to drag the *Three Sisters* and *The Cherry Orchard* out of himself. Ill health undoubtedly played a role, but there is reason to think that the feeling of being watched as he worked, of no longer being alone in his room, was implicated as well. Of course, writing a play is never as private an act as writing a story or a novel. As he works, the playwright feels a crowd of actors, directors, scenery designers, costumers, lighting specialists, and sometimes even an audience at his back. He is never alone, and he evidently likes the company. But, just as Chekhov never resolved his ambivalence toward actual guests, so he never resolved his ambivalence toward the imaginary figures who, peering over his shoulders when he wrote for the theater, inhibited him as he was not inhibited when he wrote stories. (In 1886, though, when his stories first began attracting notice, he reported a similar feeling of invasion to his friend Viktor Bilibin: "Formerly, when I didn't know that they read my tales and passed judgment on them, I wrote serenely, just the way I eat pancakes; now, I'm afraid when I write.") The theater drew and repelled Chekhov in equal measure. When, in 1898, he was approached by Nemerovich-Danchenko of the newly formed Moscow Art Theater, for permission to perform *The Seagull,* he refused. He had sworn off the theater. As Nemerovich-Danchenko reported in his memoirs, "he neither wished nor did he have the strength to undergo the great agitation of the theater that had occasioned him so much pain." Nemerovich persisted, however, and prevailed. Had he not, *Three Sisters* and *The Cherry Orchard* might still be rattling around the imaginary lumber room where Chekhov stored the subjects he didn't want to "waste."

Reading Chekhov

During a torpid passage in the Petersburg *Carmen*, my mind drifted to a small, odd detail in "The Lady with the Dog." As Gurov and Anna are strolling around Yalta after they have picked each other up in the restaurant, Gurov tells her "that he had taken his degree in Arts, but had a post in a bank; that he had trained as an opera singer, but had given it up." Trained as an opera singer! After Chekhov drops this arresting piece of information about his hero, he moves on so quickly that it scarcely registers. Chekhov never returns to it; few readers of the story will recall it. Chekhov is characteristically laconic about Gurov. He doesn't even tell us why he is in Yalta. He simply deposits him there. Chekhov was always admonishing writers who sent him manuscripts to trim down their work. "Abridge, brother, abridge! Begin on the second page," he advised his brother Alexander in 1893. He may have begun "The Lady with the Dog" on his own second page, preferring a lacuna to an overlong explanation of why a healthy, youngish married man would be alone for a month at a seaside resort peopled largely by consumptives and women with symptoms of hysteria. But he pauses to tell us that Gurov is a failed artist and a reluctant bank official, and goes on to speak of his womanizing as if it were a kind of natural by-product of his antipathy to the Philistine male business world. "In the society of men, he was bored and not himself; with them, he was cold and uncommunicative, but when he was in the company of women he felt free, and knew what to say to them and how to behave; and he was at ease with them even when he was silent." Gurov speaks of women as "the lower race," but he doesn't mean it. Women represent the freedom and ease of art, as men stand for the constraint and anxiety of commerce.

But had given it up. We may assume that Gurov had abandoned his career as an opera singer because he wasn't good enough. "You can do nothing . . . if God hasn't given you the gift." God does not give the gift freely or often: the untalented will always be with us. The gift's uneven distribution within Chekhov's own family may have instilled in him his special sympathy for the have-nots of art. His brother Alexander was the conspicuous example of the failed artist whose failure was out of his hands—whose chronic whining and feeling of being cheated by life was understandable, and perhaps even fitting, in the light of his incurable talentlessness. Chekhov never wrote directly about Alexander (or any of his siblings), but in two stories he touches on the plight of the untalented in a way that may owe something to his brother's bitter situation. In "Ionitch," (1898) a young woman named Ekaterina, who has dreams of being a great pianist, returns from her studies at a conservatory knowing that "there was nothing special about me"—that she is just a provincial girl who plays the piano like other provincial girls. Faute de mieux, she tries to rekindle the interest of the district doctor she rejected during her time of grandiose ambition, but she fails, and a light goes out in her soul. At the end of the story, "she has grown visibly older, is constantly ailing, and every autumn goes to the Crimea with her mother." Similarly, in "A Dreary Story" a trusting and charming young woman named Katya goes off to pursue a career as an actress, only to return home in the bitter knowledge that she has no talent. She, too, suffers a disappointment in love, and when we last see her she, too, is like a delicate flower that has been trampled on. The salvation through prosaic work that characters like Laevsky and Sonya and Asorin find seems to be out of the reach of those who mistakenly aspire to become artists. (In *The Seagull,* Nina, who in many ways resembles Katya, and has similar trying adventures in art and love, finally succeeds in becoming an artist, because she does have the gift. Both Katya and Nina are believed to be based on Lydia Mizinova, one of the women with whose affections Chekhov trifled, and whose ambitions as a singer were not realized.) Chekhov's sympathy for the artistically underpowered does not extend to the pretentious. He had little patience with those who, in the face of the glaring evidence of their ordinariness, believe themselves to be exceptional. In "The Grasshopper" (1892), Chekhov draws a mordant portrait of a pretty young dilettante named Olga Ivanovna, married to a modest but highly regarded doctor and scientist named Osip Stepanitch

Dymov, who fancies herself an artist and avidly collects celebrities in the art, literary, and theatrical worlds. She patronizes her husband and drifts into an affair with one of the artist celebrities, a painter named Ryabovsky. Only when it is too late—when her husband is dying of diphtheria, contracted from a patient—does she realize that it is Dymov who is the great man, and she and her celebrities are pathetic nonentities. There is a scene no one but Chekhov could have written, in which Dymov, bearing a package of caviar, cheese, and white salmon, arrives at his rented summer cottage looking forward to a nice evening with his wife, whom he has not seen for two weeks. He finds Olga not at home and the cottage overrun with her artistes. When she finally appears, she sends the tired and hungry Dymov back to the city for a pink dress she wants to wear to a wedding the next day. Dymov obediently gets back on the train and the artistes eat the caviar, cheese, and white salmon. Olga is one of the most flawed, though by no means most hateful, of Chekhov's women. She is foolish rather than malevolent—a goose rather than a snake. As Dymov lies dying, she achieves a tragic understanding of her weakness and of her missed opportunities: "She seemed to herself horrible and disgusting," and "she had a dull, despondent feeling and a conviction that her life was spoilt, and that there was no setting it right anyhow."

Twelve

In a first-class compartment of the train bearing me from St. Petersburg to Moscow—the Petersburg-Moscow Express, on which Anna Karenina traveled, carrying her red bag—I looked out the window at a rain-drenched landscape of birches and evergreens and occasionally glanced at the fat young man who lay sleeping on the seat opposite, less than two feet away. He slept for almost the entire five-hour journey, waking only to eat a meal brought by a woman attendant. As he ate, he did not once meet my gaze, and I had the feeling that his long sleep was in part or perhaps even wholly induced by a profound, helpless bashfulness.

As a literary pilgrimage this one, of course, was even more absurd than the trip to Oreanda. Anna's first-class compartment could not have been anything like the one the fat young man and I occupied, about which there was nothing first-class. Its furnishings were cheap and ugly relics of the Soviet period. The food, served in plastic containers, was gray and inedible. And yet there was a feeling here of something comfortable and familiar. Outside it was raw and wet; here it was warm and cozy. My seat—a high, narrow banquette equipped with a mattress covered with a printed cloth, and a plump large pillow—was agreeable to curl up on. It resembled the high bed on which the engineer Asorin naps, in the warm, cozy house of Bragin, after his transformative dinner. In his stories, Chekhov liked to contrast the harsh weather of God's world with the kindlier climate of man's shelters from it. He liked to bring characters out of blizzards and rain storms into warm, snug interiors. In "Gooseberries," Burkin, a schoolteacher, and Ivan Ivanovitch, a veterinarian, have got caught in a downpour while out walking, and arrive drenched and muddy and cross at the house of a landowner named Alehin, who lives alone and welcomes them gladly. After bathing, "when the lamp was lighted in the big drawing-room upstairs, and Burkin and Ivan Ivanovitch, attired in silk dressing gowns and warm slippers, were sitting in armchairs; and . . . [the servant] lovely Pelagea, stepping noiselessly on the carpet and smiling softly, handed tea and jam on a tray," Ivan Ivanovitch tells the story that gives "Gooseberries" its name.

"Gooseberries" is the second in a series of three loosely connected stories-within-stories (the outer stories have the same main characters) that Chekhov wrote in the summer of 1898—stories, as it develops, that do not celebrate the hearth but, on the contrary, constitute a three-part parable about the *perils* of staying warm and safe, and thereby missing what is worthwhile in life, if not life itself. In each instance the pleasant outer story of safe refuge has an ironic relationship to a disturbing inner story of wasted life. Chekhov hated to be cold and loved to be warm, but he knew that the payoff was in the cold. This is why he went to Sakhalin. This is why when he was in lush, semitropical Yalta he longed for the austere, icy Moscow spring.

In the first story of the series, "The Man in a Case," Burkin tells Ivan Ivanovitch—they have found shelter in a barn after a day of hunting—the tragicomic tale of a Greek teacher named Byelikov, who "displayed a constant and insurmountable impulse to wrap himself in a covering, to make himself, so to speak, a case which would isolate him and protect him from external influences. Reality irritated him, frightened him, kept him in continual agitation, and, perhaps to justify his timidity, his aversion for the actual, he always praised the past and what had never existed; and even the classical languages which he taught were in reality for him galoshes and umbrellas in which he sheltered himself from real life." When a bit of actuality—a small loss of face—penetrates his defenses, Byelikov cannot survive it. He takes to his bed and dies within a month.

In "Gooseberries," the aversion for the actual is illustrated by Ivan Ivanovitch's younger brother, Nikolai, a government clerk, who lives wrapped in a cocoon of longing for a small country estate, fitted out not only with the usual amenities—kitchen garden, duck pond, servants' quarters—but with a stand of gooseberry bushes. Achieving this gemütlich fantasy becomes an obsession, driving him to extremes of miserliness and avarice. He marries an elderly and ugly widow for her money, and keeps her on such short rations that she dies three years later. Now, at last, he can buy his estate, a charmless place without a gooseberry on it. However, he plants twenty gooseberry bushes and settles into the life of a country squire. Ivan Ivanovitch comes for a visit and finds his brother living like an escapee from *Dead Souls*—fat, uncouth, complacent, putting on airs, spouting platitudes about the management of the peasants. A servant brings a plate of sour, unripe berries—the first harvest from the new bushes—and Nikolai greedily eats them, as though they were the finest fruit of ancient bushes. Watching him, Ivan Ivanovitch has an epiphany, which he relates to Burkin and Alehin: Like Nikolai, he says, we are all insulated against reality. "We do not see and we do not hear those who suffer, and what is terrible in life goes on somewhere behind the scenes. . . . Everything is quiet and peaceful, and nothing protests but mute statistics: so many people gone out of their minds, so many gallons of vodka drunk, so many children dead from malnutrition. And this order of things is evidently necessary; evidently the happy man feels at ease only because the unhappy bear their burdens in silence, and without that silence happiness would be impossible."

He goes on:

> There ought to be behind the door of every happy, contented man someone standing with a hammer continually reminding him with a tap that there are unhappy people; that however happy he may be, life will show her laws sooner or later, trouble will come for him—disease, poverty, losses, and no one will see or hear, just as now he neither sees nor hears others.

Ivan Ivanovitch goes on in this didactic vein, ending with a plea for activism: "Do good," he says. Then Chekhov, as if anticipating the reader's reaction, writes, "Ivan Ivanovitch's story had not satisfied either Burkin or Alehin. . . . It was dreary to listen to the story of the poor clerk who ate gooseberries. They felt inclined, for some reason, to talk about elegant people, about women."

The final story, "About Love," narrated the next day by Alehin during lunch, satisfies this inclination. This time, the aversion for the actual takes the form of renunciation. It is a fragment of Alehin's autobiography. Several years before, he and a young woman named Anna Alexyevna, who was married to a good but dull man, had met and fallen in love.

However, unlike Gurov and Anna Sergeyevna (whom, in her delicate charm, Anna Alexyevna resembles), Alehin and Anna Alexyevna did not act on their feelings. For years they suppressed them, Alehin playing the part of the friend of the family, the bachelor uncle to the children, and Anna maintaining the appearance of the devoted wife. Only when the husband was taking up a new post in a distant region and Alehin came to say good-bye to Anna Alexyevna on the train did they finally acknowledge their love.

When our eyes met in the compartment, our spiritual fortitude deserted us both; I took her in my arms, she pressed her face to my breast, and tears flowed from her eyes. Kissing her face, her shoulders, her hands, wet with tears—oh, how unhappy we were—I confessed my love for her, and with a burning pain in my heart I realized how unnecessary, how petty, and how deceptive all that had hindered us from loving was. I understood that when you love you must either, in your reasonings about that love, start from what is highest—from what is more important than happiness and unhappiness, sin or virtue in their accepted meaning—or you must not reason at all.

I kissed her for the last time, pressed her hand, and parted forever. The train had already started. I went into the next compartment—it was empty—and until I reached the next station I sat there crying.

Alehin, though hardly a caricature like the Greek master or the squire brother, shares their existential malady. Like the coat and galoshes in which Byelikov encases himself and the fantasy with which the brother protects himself from the real, his attachment to conventional morality condemns him to his life of quiet desperation. A fourth desperate life—Anna Alexyevna's—is shown encasing itself in the padding of nervous illness; the train that bears her away is taking her to a transitional rest cure in the Crimea. When Chekhov wrote "The Lady with the Dog," he doubtless remembered her.

The three encased men of the trilogy are not the first (or the last) such in Chekhov's work. A predecessor is Dr. Andrey Yefimitch Ragin, the hero of "Ward No. 6," written six years earlier. Ragin is a much more fully developed example of a man who insulates himself from reality, and "Ward No. 6" is a masterpiece. But Chekhov was habitually reluctant to let go of a theme, and his compulsion to rework it in many variations is a signature of his work. It is also an aid to the critic. The ceaseless amplifications are a kind of message about meaning.

The meaning of "Ward No. 6" expands when the story is read in the light of the trilogy. Conventionally, it is read as a work of powerful social protest, a political fable whose horrifying mental ward stands for the repressive czarist state. In its rendering of suffering, this short work of fiction achieves what Chekhov's wordy factual book about Sakhalin (which he was still trying to write when he wrote "Ward No. 6") cannot. The factual work is like a photograph of a person taken from far away; "Ward No. 6" is a close-up, with all the pores and lines showing. *The Island of Sakhalin* prods and pokes; "Ward No. 6" stabs.

The story begins with a description of the repulsive outbuilding in which five lunatics are imprisoned. With a few strokes, Chekhov creates a place of such disgusting squalor and stench that the reader himself wants to flee from it. The lunatics receive no treatment. Their only human contact is with a guard named Nikita, who "belongs to the class of simple-hearted, practical, and dull-witted people, prompt in carrying out orders, who like discipline better than anything in the world, and so are convinced that it is their duty to beat people." Nikita's "fists are vigorous" and he "showers blows on the face, on the chest, on the back, on whatever comes first." The ward is part of a provincial hospital that is itself a hell. Ragin has been the chief of the hospital for some years. He is intelligent and decent but helplessly ineffectual, yet another of Chekhov's good men who cannot make good. He "had no strength of will nor belief in his right to organize an intelligent and honest life around him. He was absolutely unable to give orders, to forbid things, or to insist." Although Ragin immediately realizes that the hospital is a place of evil and should be closed down, he takes no action.

He sinks into a life of escape from life. He has less and less to do with the hospital and never goes into the mental ward. He does almost nothing at all, in fact. He reads and talks to the town's postmaster, Mihail Averyanitch, "the only man in town whose society did not bore [him]" but who is actually a bore and a cheat. Then one day chance brings Ragin to Ward 6 and into conversation with a thirty-three-year-old paranoid inmate named Ivan Dmitritch Gromov, who (unlike the four other inmates) is of noble birth.

In April 1892, Chekhov described "Ward No. 6" to Avilova—surely not without irony—as "very boring . . . since woman and the element of love are entirely absent from it." (He added, "I can't bear such tales, and as for writing this one, I did it inadvertently somehow, and frivolously.") In fact, however, the element of love is very much present in the story. How else to describe the pleasure and excitement aroused in Ragin by his encounter with Gromov, a genuinely interesting and appealing man, someone with whom he can finally engage? Ragin starts coming regularly to Ward 6 and holding philosophical debates with Gromov. He comes alive. Gromov is a precursor of R. D. Laing's sane madman in a mad world. His paranoia is a too acute awareness of the wrongs of the world. Ragin takes the position that active efforts to alleviate the wrongs of the world are useless and pointless, since we all will die. He advocates a stoic indifference to external reality. "There is no real difference between a warm, snug study and this ward," he says. "A man's peace and contentment do not lie outside a man, but in himself." The cold and starved and beaten Gromov wonderfully replies, "You should go and preach that philosophy in Greece, where it's warm and fragrant with the scent of pomegranates, but here it is not suited to the climate. . . . Diogenes did not need a study or a warm habitation; it's hot there without. You can lie in your tub and eat oranges and olives. But bring him to Russia to live: he'd be begging to be let indoors in May, let alone December. He'd be doubled up with the cold." As the conversation continues, the madman eloquently challenges the sane doctor's quietism, and draws a devastating portrait of him:

> "You are naturally a flabby, lazy man, and so you have
> tried to arrange your life so that nothing should disturb
> you or make you move. You have handed over your
> work to the assistant and the rest of the rabble while
> you sit in peace and warmth, save money, read, amuse
> yourself with reflections, with all sorts of lofty non-
> sense . . . in fact you have seen nothing of life, you
> know absolutely nothing of it, and are only theoreti-
> cally acquainted with reality. . . . You see a peasant
> beating his wife, for instance. Why interfere? Let him
> beat her, they will both die sooner or later, anyway. . . .
> A peasant woman comes with toothache . . . well, what
> of it? Pain is the idea of pain, and besides 'there is no

living in this world without illness; we shall all die, and so, go away, woman, don't hinder me from thinking and drinking vodka.' . . . We are kept here behind barred windows, tortured, left to rot; but that is very good and reasonable, because there is no difference at all between this ward and a warm snug study. A convenient philosophy. You can do nothing, and your conscience is clear, and you feel you are wise. . . . No sir, it is not philosophy, it's not thinking, it's not breadth of vision, but laziness, fakirism, drowsy stupefaction. . . ."

None of this penetrates. Ragin can only laugh with pleasure at having found such an interesting and intelligent man to talk to. "That's original," he says to Gromov of his harsh portrait. Only when he is himself thrown into the ward—this is the story's incredible plot twist, which Chekhov succeeds in making believable—does he at last confront reality. Here is the form the confrontation takes:

Nikita opened the door quickly, and roughly, with both his hands and his knee, shoved Andrey Yefimitch back, then swung his arm and punched him in the face with his fist. It seemed to Andrey Yefimitch as though a huge salt wave enveloped him from his head downwards and dragged him to the bed; there really was a salt taste in his mouth: most likely the blood was running from his teeth. He waved his arms as though he were trying to swim out and clutched at a bedstead, and at the same moment felt Nikita hit him twice on the back. . . . Then all was still, the faint moonlight came through the grating, and a shadow like a net lay on the floor. It was terrible. Andrey Yefimitch lay and held his breath: he was expecting with horror to be struck again. He felt as though someone had taken a sickle, thrust it into him, and turned it round several times in his breast and bowels. He bit the pillow from pain and clenched his teeth, and all at once through the chaos in his brain there flashed the terrible, unbearable thought that these people, who seemed now like black shadows in the moonlight, had to endure such pain day after day for years. How could it have happened that for more than twenty years he had known it and had refused to know it?

The next day, Ragin dies of a stroke, and the story ends.

Reading "Ward No. 6" as a political parable is not adequate to its power. One puts it down feeling that in writing it Chekhov had in mind nothing so local as the condition of the Russian empire. As always, it is with the human condition that he is preoccupied. "Life will show her laws sooner or later, trouble will come for [the happy, contented man]—disease, poverty, losses, and no one will see or hear, just as now he neither sees nor hears others." Nikita embodies the brutality of life itself coming at us all with its big fists. Chekhov condemns Ragin for his refusal to bestir himself on behalf of his suffering fellow men, but he also understands him. As a nonbeliever, he, too, has felt the absurdity of it all in the light of our ineluctable permanent extinction beneath the cold stars of a ten-billion-year-old universe.

In "Lights," he puts into the mouth of his reformed rake, Ananyev, a speech about the philosophy of absurdism that at once satirizes it and gives it its due.

> "I was no more than twenty-six at the time [when he seduced and betrayed the trusting Kisochka], but I knew perfectly well that life was aimless and had no meaning, that everything was a deception and an illusion, that in its essential nature and results a life of penal servitude in Sakhalin was not in any way different from a life spent in Nice, that the difference between the brain of a Kant and the brain of a fly was of no real significance. . . . I lived as though I were doing a favor to some unseen power which compelled me to live. . . . The philosophy of which we are speaking has something alluring, narcotic in its nature, like tobacco or morphia. It becomes a habit, a craving. You take advantage of every minute of solitude to gloat over thoughts of the aimlessness of life and the darkness of the grave."

To a young listener, who himself finds life absurd, and challenges a distinction that Ananyev makes between the pessimism of the old and the pessimism of the young, Ananyev replies:

The pessimism of old thinkers does not take the form of idle talk, as it does with you and me, but of Weltschmerz, of suffering; it rests in them on a Christian foundation because it is derived from love for humanity and from thoughts about humanity, and is entirely free from the egotism which is noticeable in dilettantes. You despise life because its meaning and its object are hidden from you alone, and you are afraid only of your own death, while the real thinker is unhappy because the truth is hidden from all, and he is afraid for all men.

In his stories and plays, Chekhov is afraid for all men. He was only in his twenties and thirties when he wrote most of them, but like other geniuses—especially those who die prematurely—he wrote as if he were old. Toward the end of "Ward No. 6," he veers off—as he does in other dark and terrible works, such as "Peasants" and "In the Ravine"—to rejoice for all men in the beauty of the world. There is always this amazing movement in Chekhov from the difficult and fearful to the simple and beautiful. As Ragin lies dying, Chekhov tells us, he sees "a greenness before his eyes"; then "a herd of deer, extraordinarily beautiful and graceful, of which he had been reading the day before, ran by him."

"Life is given to us only once." The line (or a variant) appears in story after story and is delivered so quietly and offhandedly that we almost miss its terror. Chekhov was never one to insist on anything. He didn't preach, or even teach. He is our poet of the provisional and fragmentary. When a story or play ends, nothing seems to be settled. "Ward No. 6," for instance, does not end with the image of the beautiful deer. Before Ragin dies another thought passes through his mind: "A peasant woman stretched out her hand to him with a registered letter. . . . Mihail Averyanitch said something, then it all vanished, and Andrey Yefimitch sank into oblivion forever." The registered letter—there is a bit of theatricality in its not being an ordinary letter—glints with meaning. What does it say? Who sent it? The ending of "Ward No. 6" inevitably evokes (and was surely influenced by) the ending of "The Death of Ivan Ilyich," but Chekhov declines to report the mystical experience that Tolstoy confidently reports his hero to have had. Chekhov enters the dying Ragin's mind, but emerges with the most laconic and incomplete of reports. Tolstoy's audacious authorial omniscience gives him his position as the greatest of the nineteenth-century Russian realists. Chekhov's experiments with authorial reticence—equally audacious in their way—point toward twentieth-century modernism.

Thirteen

In my room at the Hotel Yalta, I tried to turn on the TV, to get the news (during a telephone call to New York, I had heard that Yeltsin was about to be impeached), but could not. I called the front desk, and was told, "There is a woman on your floor. She will help you."

"What woman?"

"There is a woman on every floor, near the elevator. She will help you."

I walked down the long corridor and eventually found a room where a fat, slatternly woman with long blond hair was sitting. The room was astonishing. It had been commandeered by grape ivy vines, which trailed and twined over the walls and ceiling, forming a kind of canopy and giving everything in the room a green tinge. The vines grew from two incongruously small plastic pots on a windowsill. The paucity of soil gave the plants a leggy and slightly deprived look, but in no way diminished their will to push on and cover the world with themselves. Earlier in the day, Nina and I had seen indoor plants living under the most luxurious conditions imaginable, in the conservatory of a palace built by a Prince Volkonsky—plants with glossy dark green leaves, set in large clay pots filled with dark, rich soil. But the leggy grape ivy tended by the slatternly woman belonged to the same universe of horticulture as the glossy plants tended by professional gardeners. "All Russia is a garden," begins Trofimov's great speech in *The Cherry Orchard* about his intimations of the happiness the future will bring to his country—a speech one doesn't quite know how to listen to in the light of the catastrophe that actually befell Russia.

I told the woman my problem with the television. She nodded and went to a corner cupboard, from which she withdrew a key. She used it to lock her room before following me to my room, where she pointed out a switch I had missed. I gave her a tip, for which she thanked me profusely. I reflected that my telephone call to New York, which cost fifteen dollars, was more than a week's pay for her—and for most of the people I had met in Russia. The comparison was the sort of trite and useless rhetoric Chekhov would sometimes put in the mouth of a character whose reformist views excited his skepticism. One such reformer is the narrator of "An Anonymous Story," a confused revolutionary nobleman, who compares a dress costing four hundred rubles to the pitiful wages in kopecks of poor women. "An Anonymous Story" is a strange, febrile work that reads as if it had been written nonstop in the state of heightened consciousness that tuberculosis has been said to induce in artists. (In actuality, the story was set aside for several years after it was started.) It begins arrestingly:

> Through causes which it is not the time to go into in detail, I had to enter the service of a Petersburg official called Orlov, in the capacity of a footman. . . . I entered the service of this Orlov on account of his father, a prominent political man, whom I looked upon as a serious enemy of my cause. I reckoned that, living with the son, I should—from the conversations I would hear, and from the letters and papers I would find on the table—learn every detail of the father's plans and intentions.

But the story does not live up to its promise. For reasons one can attribute only to Chekhov's own lack of enthusiasm for revolution, the narrator loses interest in his cause, becoming exclusively preoccupied with the predicament of Orlov's beautiful young mistress, Zinaida (to whom Orlov is behaving with typical Petersburg swinishness). But the opening scenes, retailing the upper-class revolutionary's masquerade as a servant—scenes that perhaps only someone who had himself been on both sides of the class divide could have written—have a special sardonic sparkle. Chekhov wrote easily about the upper classes—the term

"Chekhovian" evokes faded nobility on decaying estates—but he evidently never forgot that he himself had not been gently reared. In a letter to Suvorin written in January 1889, he speaks of a "feeling of personal freedom" that "only recently began to develop in me," and continues:

> What writers belonging to the upper class have received from nature for nothing, plebeians acquire at the cost of their youth. Write a story of how a young man, the son of a serf, who has served in a shop, sung in a choir, been at a high school and university, who has been brought up to respect everyone of higher rank and position, to kiss priests' hands, to revere other people's ideas, to be thankful for every morsel of bread, who has been many times whipped, who has trudged from one pupil to another without galoshes, who has been used to fighting, and tormenting animals, who has liked dining with his rich relations, and been hypocritical before God and men from the mere consciousness of his own insignificance—write how this young man squeezes the slave out of himself, drop by drop, and how waking one beautiful morning he feels that he has no longer a slave's blood in his veins but a real man's.

This passage is much quoted and is generally believed to be an expression of Chekhov's free-spiritedness. In fact, it subtly enacts what it condemns; it is itself servile, unpleasantly suggesting that the plebeian is innately inferior, that he needs to expunge some noxious substance within himself before he can rise to the level of the aristocrat. The image of squeezing is unpleasant. Chekhov writes here almost like a self-loathing Jew reassuring himself that he has passed. Nowhere else in his writings does he express such sentiments. It is a moment of anxiety that has no sequel. But it is a moment—like the "Karelin's Dream" letter—that flares out of the genial documents of his life like an out-of-control fire glimpsed from a moving train.

That it was to Alexei Suvorin that this letter was addressed is surely no accident. If Chekhov loved Tolstoy better than any man, it was Suvorin with whom he felt most comfortable. Suvorin was another self-made man, and also the grandson of a serf. He was twenty-six years older than Chekhov, and the millionaire publisher of *New Times,* a right-wing daily with the largest circulation of any newspaper in Russia, as well as the owner of a large publishing house, five bookshops, and the majority of the bookstalls in Russian railway stations. In addition, he was a writer (of plays and stories) of some accomplishment. Suvorin's invitation to Chekhov in 1886 to write stories for *New Times* at the high rate of twelve kopecks a line is regarded as the fulcrum of Chekhov's artistic emergence. He had already begun to liberate himself from the humor genre; he was writing longer, nonhumorous stories for the daily *Petersburg Gazette*. But the *Gazette* paid poorly, and it was only Suvorin's offer that permitted him to cut his ties with the humor magazines and devote himself to serious fiction. Grigorovich wrote Chekhov an electrifyingly flattering letter, but it was Suvorin who created the conditions under which he could produce art.

The friendship that developed between the middle-aged magnate and the young writer aroused the sort of envy and derision such relationships do. Chekhov, of course, did not share the reactionary and anti-Semitic views of *New Times*—which only made his motives seem more suspect. (In actuality, the differences between Chekhov's and Suvorin's politics were not as great as they appeared; in private, Suvorin could evidently permit himself less objectionable views than those of his paper. In time, however, the paper's shrill anti-Dreyfusism was to put a serious strain on the friendship.) The theater critic Alexander Kugel wrote (Donald Rayfield tells us), "The way [Suvorin] entertained Chekhov, looked at him, enveloped him with his eyes, reminded one somehow of a rich man showing off his new 'kept woman.' " Along the same lines (according to Simmons), Shcheglov quoted a Petersburg literary rival of Chekhov as saying: "Chekhov is a Suvorin kept woman!" This was not so: Chekhov took no money from Suvorin beyond his earnings and an occasional loan (which he always punctually repaid). Suvorin's hospitality to him at his mansion in St. Petersburg (Nelly pointed it out to me during a tour of the city—a large red stone building of a sturdy Victorian cast) and at his estate in the Crimean resort town of Feodosia was reciprocated by Chekhov in the country houses he rented before buying Melikhovo, and then at Melikhovo (which, much to his sorrow, Suvorin didn't like). Everything was extremely correct in this regard. (How far Chekhov was from sponging off Suvorin can be inferred from a letter he wrote to his sister while traveling in Europe with Suvorin: he wistfully noted how cheap the trip would have been had he not had to stay in the fancy hotels and eat in the expensive restaurants that Suvorin favored.)

When the two men weren't together, they faithfully—you could almost say obsessively—corresponded. We have only Chekhov's side of the correspondence. Simmons reports that when Chekhov died Suvorin turned over Chekhov's letters to Maria in exchange for his own. The latter were never seen again, so we don't know what tone Suvorin adopted toward his protégé. But from Chekhov's letters we may gather that he and Suvorin were more like a father and son who adored each other than like a kept woman and her wealthy protector. Suvorin was the generous, appreciative, worldly, bookish father Chekhov should have had, rather than the narrow, cruel tyrant he got. The relationship, as Rayfield has characterized it, was "one of the most fertile in Russian literature." Olga, who was perpetually reproaching Chekhov for the brevity and levity of his letters to her ("Write me a beautiful, sincere letter and don't take refuge in jokes, as you so often do. Write what you feel"), would have killed for one of Chekhov's beautiful, sincere letters to Suvorin. "You complain of the shortness of my letters," Chekhov wrote to Olga in 1901, and lamely explained, "My dear, my handwriting is small." To Suvorin he wrote letters that ended only when his fingers began to ache. "In case of trouble or boredom where am I to go? Whom am I to turn to?" he wrote in the summer of 1893 when Suvorin was about to go abroad. "There are devilish moods when one wants to talk and write, yet I don't correspond with anybody but you, and there is nobody whom I talk with for any length of time."

But even to Suvorin Chekhov refused the ultimate epistolary satisfaction, the unconditional declaration of love. "This doesn't mean that you are better than all those whom I know," he felt constrained to add, "but it does mean that I have grown used to you and that you are the only one with whom I feel free." A number of memoirists have written of Chekhov's inability to get close to anyone. One must always be skeptical of such an observation, since it can simply describe the relationship of the subject and the memoirist, and not necessarily apply to the subject's other relationships. In Chekhov's case, though, the observation comes from a variety of sources, and it seems to fit. The consensus is that Chekhov was extremely charming to everyone and close to no one—not even to Suvorin, to whom he came closer to being close than to anyone else. In his last years, weakened by illness, he married a woman with whom—had he been healthy—he probably would have broken, as he had broken with all the other women in his life. It was not in his character to give his heart away.

It was also not his habit to give himself away in his work; he was not a confessional writer. But in one story at least he may have practiced a veiled form of autobiography. That story is "Kashtanka" (1887), narrated from the point of view of a female dog, and presented as a story for children. In fact, it is a dark, strange, rather horrible (as well as wonderful) fable that I, for one, would never read to a child. The story reverses the usual formula of the well-treated animal who is wrested from a comfortable home and made to endure cruel hardship until it is finally reunited with its humane original master or mistress. Kashtanka is a hungry and ill-treated animal who gets lost, is adopted by a kindly man, and then is reunited (by her own choice) with her abusive original owner. The kindly man finds Kashtanka shivering in the doorway of a bar during a snowstorm, and takes her home and feeds her. He is an animal trainer who has a circus act performed by a cat, a gander, and a pig. He adopts Kashtanka, starts teaching her tricks, for which she proves to have great aptitude, and one day brings her to the circus to perform in the act with the others. The original owner, an alcoholic carpenter, happens to be in the audience with his son, and when the two of them call to her, Kashtanka leaps out of the ring to go to them, and unhesitatingly, and even joyfully, resumes her life of privation.

Chekhov prepares for the ending by depicting the household of the kindly master as a faintly sinister place. Kashtanka and the cat and the gander are kept in a room always identified as the little room with dirty wallpaper. An uneasiness is always present, a kind of uncanniness that reaches a climax one night when the gander utters a horrible shriek and then pathetically dies, as the dog howls and the standoffish cat huddles against her. When read as a parable of alienation—a case study of homesickness—the dog's return to the original master takes on a sort of tragic inevitability. We know that the sleek, well-groomed animal Kashtanka has become under the care of the kindly circus master will soon again be a bag of bones, beaten by the carpenter and tortured by the son. But she will be cured of her unease; she will be where she belongs, leading her own proper life, rather than a life that is not really hers.

When Chekhov wrote "Kashtanka," he was himself living an alien new life. In 1886 he had been abruptly catapulted from obscurity to celebrity. He had been taken up by literary Russia's greatest circus master and pronounced a genuine artist. ("I want to make an artiste of you," Kashtanka's new master says to her. "Do you want to be an artiste?" And, after seeing her perform—as if he had Grigorovich's letter to Chekhov in front of him—he exclaims, "It's talent! It's talent! Unquestionable talent! You will certainly be successful!") But being a part of Suvorin's circus act made Chekhov as tense as it made him happy. We have seen his dismay at no longer being able to produce stories the way he eats pancakes. His letters of the period have a feverish, manic quality, he seems all over the place in them, like an excited, unsure puppy. He is alternately boastful and fearful. Chekhov's letters now also begin to express an ambivalence toward writing that was to remain with him. They suggest that the literary artist, like the animal performer, is doing something unnatural, almost unseemly. Making art goes against nature. People, like animals, weren't made to perform such feats. If life is given only once, it shouldn't be spent writing. Chekhov would often talk of idleness as the only form of happiness. He said he loved nothing better than fishing. At the same time, like Trigorin in *The Seagull,* he was afflicted with the writer's compulsion to perpetually, ruthlessly sift life for material, to be writing something in his head all the time.

If it was Chekhov's fate to be a reluctant literary performer, it was also his fate to remain with his impossible "original owners." His adoption by Suvorin was as inconsequential as Kashtanka's adventure with the circusmaster. Chekhov's autocratic father, the kindly, uneducated mother, who had been helpless to defend him against the father, the feckless older brothers, the not brilliant younger ones, and the unmarried Maria were the people to whom he felt connected. All the rest were "customers," to use Kashtanka's term for outsiders. The friendly reserve he maintained toward outsiders was the outward token of the iron tie to the family. Literally as well as figuratively, Chekhov never left home. Whatever he meant by his new "feeling of freedom," he didn't mean the usual young person's leavetaking of his family. He kept his parents with him in Moscow and Melikhovo, and, after his father's death, in 1889, he brought his mother to his house in Yalta. Maria, too, was always with him. According to her memoirs (written in old age), she turned down the proposal of an attractive man named Alexander Smagin, "because I could not do anything that would cause unpleasantness to my brother, upset the customary course of his life, and deprive him of the conditions for creative work which I always tried to provide." Chekhov had merely remained silent when she announced her intention of marrying, Maria reports, but this was enough for her to break with Smagin. (Having sacrificed herself for her brother, she was understandably put out when he himself married; however, she remained a fixture in the household, and she and Olga were friends into old age.) Chekhov was as closemouthed about his relationship to his sister as he was about his relationship to any other woman. The letters he wrote to her when he traveled are easy and natural (as are his letters to his brothers). But what the relationship was like—what its tone was, what its themes were—remains among the secrets of the nest.

When I turned on the television set in my room at the Hotel Yalta, I had the choice of four channels, two of them in Ger-

man. All were blurred. I chose one of the Russian stations,
which was showing an American movie. Instead of being
dubbed, the film was shown with the sound very low, almost inaudible, and with a loud overvoice translating the
characters' speech into Russian. By listening very hard, I
could make out some of what the characters were saying.
The film seemed to be about a mortally ill child whose father takes him to a desert where God has instructed the father to build a stone altar. The child's mother, back home,
sends a friend to beg for his return. The father refuses.
"What shall I tell Caroline?" the friend asks. I did not need
to strain my ears for the reply: "Tell her that I love her." At
the end, the sky opens, lightning flashes over the altar, and
the miracle occurs: the boy is cured. In Chekhov, there are
no miraculous cures. When characters are sick, they die. It is
hard to think of a Chekhov play or story in which no death
occurs (or over which, having already occurred, it doesn't
hover, as the drowning of Ranevskaya's son hovers over *The
Cherry Orchard*). Death is the hinge on which the work
swings.

"The Lady with the Dog" is an apparent exception—no
one in the story dies or has died. And yet death is in the air.
Gurov's spiritual journey—his transformation from a con-
noisseur of women to a man tenderly devoted to a single ordinary woman—is a journey of withdrawal from life. His
life as a womanizer wasn't nice, but it was vital; his secret
"real life" in the Moscow hotel has a ghostly quality. He

and Anna are like people for whom "the eternal sleep await-
ing us" has already begun. Anna's Yalta hotel room smelled
of a scent from a Japanese shop, and there was a watermelon on the table; the room at the Slaviansky Bazaar is
odorless, and there is nothing to eat. Anna Sergeyevna is
pale, and dressed in gray ("his favorite gray dress"); Gurov,
catching a glimpse of himself in the mirror, sees that his hair
is gray. The color of ashes has already begun to infiltrate the
story. When Gurov—like Orpheus descending to the under-
world—traveled to S——, he found a long gray fence in front
of Anna Sergeyevna's house and in his hotel room "the floor
was covered with gray army cloth, and on the table was an
inkstand, gray with dust." (Something stirs in one's memory
here. One recalls that at the end of "A Dreary Story" the
dying professor stays in a hotel in Harkov, where he sleeps
under "an unfamiliar gray quilt" and peevishly remarks,
"It's so gray here—such a gray town.") In the Moscow hotel
room, Gurov notes that "he had grown so much older, so
much plainer during the last few years," and goes on to ob-
serve of Anna Sergeyevna, "The shoulders on which his
hands rested were warm and quivering. He felt compassion
for this life still so warm and lovely, but probably already
not far from beginning to fade and wither like his own." He
sounds almost as if he were speaking of a corpse. In Yalta,
only a year or two earlier, he had been struck by Anna's
youth, by "how lately she had been a girl at school doing

lessons like his own daughter." (She was twenty-two.) He had (twice) noted her schoolgirlish "diffidence" and "angularity." But now this woman who could be his daughter is on the verge of "fading" and "withering." His actual daughter accompanies him on his walk to his tryst in the Moscow hotel. What is Chekhov getting at with his theme of the two daughters? Is he anticipating Freud's mythopoetic reading of *King Lear* in "The Theme of the Three Caskets"? Does Anna Sergeyevna—like Cordelia—represent the Goddess of Death? Has Gurov, like the professor in Harkov (and Chekhov in Yalta), come to the end of the line? We do not ask such questions of the other Russian realists, but Chekhov's strange, coded works almost force us to sound them for hidden meanings. Chekhov's irony and good sense put a brake on our speculations. We don't want to get too fancy. But we don't want to miss the clues that Chekhov has scattered about his garden and covered with last year's leaves. These leaves are fixtures of Chekhov's world (I have encountered them in the gardens of no other writer), and exemplify Chekhov's way of endowing some small quiet natural phenomenon with metaphorical meaning. One hears them crunch underfoot as one walks in the allée where this year's leaves have already sprouted.

Bibliography

CHEKHOV BIOGRAPHY AND CRITICISM CITED IN THE TEXT

Avilov, Lydia. *Chekhov in My Life.* Translated and with an introduction by David Magarshack. New York, 1950.

Callow, Philip. *Chekhov: The Hidden Ground.* Chicago: Ivan R. Dee, 1998.

Carver, Raymond. *Where I'm Calling From: New and Selected Stories.* 1988. New York: Vintage, 1989.

Chudakov, A. P. *Chekhov's Poetics.* Translated by Edwina Jannie Cruise and Donald Dragt. Ann Arbor, Michigan: Ardis, 1983.

Finke, Michael. "Chekhov's 'Steppe': A Metapoetic Journey." In *Anton Chekhov Rediscovered: A Collection of New Studies with a Comprehensive Bibliography,* edited by Savely Senderovich and Munir Sendich. East Lansing, Michigan: Russian Language Journal, 1987.

Freud, Sigmund. "The Theme of the Three Caskets." Standard edition, vol. 13. London: Hogarth Press.

Gilles, Daniel. *Chekhov: Observer Without Illusion.* Translated by Charles Lam Markmann. New York: Funk and Wagnalls, 1967.

Jackson, Robert Louis, editor. *Reading Chekhov's Text*. Evanston, Illinois: Northwestern University Press, 1993.

———"Dostoevsky in Chekhov's Garden of Eden—'Because of Little Apples,' " in *Dialogue with Dostoevsky*. Stanford, California: Stanford University Press, 1993.

Karlinsky, Simon. "Huntsmen, Birds, Forests, and Three Sisters," in *Chekhov's Great Plays: A Critical Anthology*. Edited and with an introduction by Jean-Pierre Barricelli. New York: New York University, 1981.

Karlinsky, Simon, and Michael Henry Heim. *Anton Chekhov's Life and Thought: Selected Letters and Commentary*. Translation by Heim in collaboration with Karlinsky; selection, introduction, and commentary by Karlinsky. Evanston, Illinois: Northwestern University Press, 1973.

Magarshack, David. *Chekhov: A Life*. New York: Grove, 1952.

Mihailovic, Alexandar. "Eschatology and Entombment in 'Ionich' " in *Reading Chekhov's Text*, edited by Robert Louis Jackson. Evanston, Illinois: Northwestern University Press, 1993.

Morson, Gary Saul. "Prosaic Chekhov: Metadrama, the Intelligentsia, and Uncle Vanya." *TriQuarterly* 80 (winter 1990–91).

Nabokov, Vladimir. "Anton Chekhov." In *Lectures on Russian Literature*. New York: Harcourt Brace, 1981.

Pitcher, Harvey. *Chekhov's Leading Lady: A Portrait of the Actress Olga Knipper*. 1979. New York: Franklin Watts, 1980.

Pritchett, V. S. *Chekhov: A Spirit Set Free*. New York: Random House, 1988.

Rabeneck, L. L. "Posledniye minuty Chekhova." *Vozrozhdeniye,* vol. 84. Paris, December 1958.

———" 'Serdtse Chekhova.' " *Vozrozhdeniye,* vol. 92. Paris, August 1959.

Rayfield, Donald. *Anton Chekhov: A Life.* New York: Henry Holt, 1997.

de Sherbinin, Julie W. *Chekhov and Russian Religious Culture: The Poetics of the Marian Paradigm.* Evanston, Illinois: Northwestern University Press, 1997.

Simmons, Ernest J. *Chekhov: A Biography.* Boston: Atlantic Monthly Press, 1962.

Toumanova, Nina Andronikova. *Anton Chekhov: The Voice of Twilight Russia.* New York: Columbia University Press, 1937.

Troyat, Henri. *Chekhov.* Translated from the French by Michael Henry Heim. New York: Dutton, 1986.

Turkov, Andrei, editor. *Anton Chekhov and His Times.* Translated by Cynthia Carlile and Sharon McKee. Fayetteville: University of Arkansas Press, 1995.

TRANSLATIONS USED IN THE TEXT

Benedetti, Jean, editor and translator. *Dear Writer, Dear Actress: The Love Letters of Anton Chekhov and Olga Knipper.* New York: Ecco, 1996.

Dunnigan, Ann, translator. *Chekhov: The Major Plays.* Foreword by Robert Brustein.

Friedland, Louis S. *Letters on the Short Story, the Drama, and Other Literary Topics.* New York: Dover, 1966.

Bibliography

Garnett, Constance, translator. *Four Great Plays by Chekhov*. New York: Bantam Books, 1958.

———, translator. *The Tales of Chekhov*. 13 volumes. New York: Ecco, 1984.

———, translator. *Letters of Anton Chekhov to His Family and Friends with Biographical Sketch*. New York: Macmillan, 1920.

———, translator. *The Letters of Anton Pavlovitch Tchekhov to Olga Leonardovna Knipper*. New York: Doran, 1924.

Karlinsky, Simon, and Michael Henry Heim. *Anton Chekhov's Life and Thought: Selected Letters and Commentary*. Translation by Heim in collaboration with Karlinsky; selection, introduction, and commentary by Karlinsky. Evanston, Illinois: Northwestern University Press, 1973.

Terpak, Luba, and Michael Terpak, translators. *The Island of Sakhalin*. Introduction by Ratushinskaya. London: The Folio Society, 1989.

Yarmolinsky, Avrahm, translator. *Letters of Anton Chekhov*. New York: Viking, 1973.

———, editor. *The Portable Chekhov*. Translated by Constance Garnett, Bernard G. Gurney, and Yarmolinsky. New York: Viking Penguin, 1947.

———, translator. *The Unknown Chekhov: Stories and Other Writings*. New York: Noonday, 1954; Ecco, 1984.

ABOUT THE TYPE

This book was set in Sabon, a typeface designed by well-known German typographer Jan Tschichold (1902–74). Sabon's design is based upon the original letter forms of Claude Garamond and was created specifically to be used for three sources: foundry type for hand composition, Linotype, and Monotype. Tschichold named his typeface for the famous Frankfurt typefounder Jacques Sabon, who died in 1580.

Printed in the United States
by Baker & Taylor Publisher Services